AT ROMMEL'S SIDE

AT ROMMEL'S SIDE

The lost letters of

Hans-Joachim Schraepler

Edited by
Hans-Albrecht Max Schraepler

Introduction by
Dennis Showalter

Frontline Books, London

At Rommel's Side: The Lost Letters of Hans-Joachim Schraepler

This edition published in 2009 by Frontline Books, an imprint of
Pen & Sword Books Limited, 47 Church Street, Barnsley, S. Yorkshire, S70 2AS
www.frontline-books.com

© ÉDITIONS PRIVAT 2007
Translation © Hans-Albrecht Schraepler, 2009
This edition © Pen & Sword Books Limited, 2009

ISBN: 978-1-84832-538-8

Publishing History
Mon Père, l'Aide de Camp du Général Rommel was first published in French by
Éditions Privat in 2007. This is the first English-language edition of the text and
includes a new introduction by Dennis Showalter.

A CIP data record for this title is available from the British Library.

For more information on our books, please visit
www.frontline-books.com, email info@frontline-books.com
or write to us at the above address.

Typeset by Palindrome
Printed in the UK by the MPG Books Group

War is the main topic of nations; it is the place where death and life are decided.

It is the way of one's own survival or of one's own end. It should not be treated carelessly.

The war is subject to five factors to be included in the analytical calculation of the balance of powers.

The first factor is the virtue, the second the climate, topography the third, the fourth the command, the fifth organisation . . .

Sun Tsu: army general in China and philosopher, about 500 BC,
The Art of War, chapter I

Contents

Foreword

I discovered the bundled letters of my father, Lieutenant Colonel Hans-Joachim Schraepler, adjutant of the Deutsches Afrika Korps, after my mother died in 2001. He wrote his first letter from Tripoli on 20 February 1941, his last on 9 December 1941. He wrote to my mother almost every day, either early in the morning, at noon, late in the evening or in the middle of the night, whenever time and fighting at the front permitted. Altogether I found more than 400 pages.

His last words were deeply marked by the depressing withdrawal of the Afrika Korps under British pressure and by the information that his wife's cousin, General Walter Neumann-Silkow, had succumbed to the serious wounds received the day before.

I knew, of course, that my father had joined the cavalry of the Weimar Republic after finishing school, progressing in his military career in Pomerania, a former Prussian province, during a politically difficult period for Germany and Europe. North Africa was an unknown continent for him and his comrades. His letters reveal the importance of his conservative and traditional background to his ability to withstand the hard and exhausting conditions of war in the desert.

The letters also show his doubts about the policy of the Berlin regime after the invasion of the Soviet Union. Today we know that, despite initial successes, the war against Stalin would not be finished by the winter and the country had no intention of surrendering. For my father, as for many others, the realisation of this was crushing.

His letters were often written in a hurry or in sections, depending on the changing war situation. But they were always full of information about the war in the desert, Rommel's leadership, British strategy and his observations as an adjutant in the Afrika Korps functioning as he did between the staff and fighting troops. By the end of 1941 he rarely found calm moments to inform my mother about his condition or to note down his reflections as the situation at the front continued to deteriorate. The German troops suffered from lack of supplies on the ground and British supremacy on land, at sea and in the air.

His letters are informative and precise, and mention interesting details without getting bogged down. They also indicate his professional experience and present military and strategic views which, above all, show his loyalty to Rommel; and they do not hide a certain reserve regarding the regime in Berlin, as he is conscious, without mentioning it, of his 'oath of fidelity to Führer and Reich' (made on the instructions of the minister of war of 2 August 1934).

They touch on topics like the strategic difficulties of the front in North Africa that were characterised by the particular context of North Africa in the international war. The letters are unique documents: they describe Rommel, the commanding general of the Afrika Korps, later of the Panzergruppe 'Afrika', without neglecting the situation at the front, which had the distinction of being the only deployment of German troops on another continent during World War II on the one hand, yet which was both geographically close and strategically important.

He describes not only the phases of the war front in Libya in 1941, the lengthy and unsuccessful siege of Tobruk and the famous *Panzerschlacht* (tank battle) of Sollum, but he also assesses the personality and strategy of Rommel, criticising him if he had reasons to, repeatedly mentioning how hard the demands of this war were for each soldier in the merciless desert without any natural protection or other options.

I found his assessment of the British adversary particularly interesting: he saw that their war stratagems were not always recognised by the German side, and that it was their need to defend the interests of the British Empire in the Mediterranean – including the Suez Canal and the Red Sea needed for access to the Indian Ocean and the British colonies – that was motivating the war in North Africa. He realised that this was in contrast to the way Berlin politics continually revised war ambitions in other theatres.

My father did not hesitate to express his concern about the outcome of the North Africa campaign. It started to come up in his letters a few weeks after the attack on the Soviet Union in June 1941. Overall, I feel that in his letters my father knew exactly what he was talking about and to whom he had been writing such frank letters.

The letters are bold. They are even courageous. Only a few of his letters show the familiar signs of censorship. Owing to his position in the Afrika Korps, my father was always well informed and he constantly identified comrades leaving for Germany to whom he could entrust his letters on some occasions to avoid the official field post.

Almost every letter confirmed my impression of his deep understanding of military affairs, from his time in a regiment of cavalry of the Reichswehr, the army of the Weimar Republic, when it was confronting deep changes in Germany after the end of World War I; and of his strong beliefs as officer and soldier: his loyalty to Germany, his affiliation to the Wehrmacht, his relationship with his comrades and his feelings for his family.

When reading the letter dated 25 August 1941, I remembered a conversation with my mother. I had asked her how her husband, my father, would have accepted the end of World War II with its far-reaching consequences for Germany, Europe and the world on the whole. She seemed to be surprised, for she hesitated a short moment before giving an answer. She looked at me and told me that she believed that he would not have regretted having chosen a career in the army; but he would have regretted belonging to a Wehrmacht whose supreme command had forgotten its role and function in a state where tradition, national feelings and progress are linked for the benefit of the country.

Hans-Albrecht Max Schraepler

Introduction

A staff officer's job is seldom equated with any risks more serious than a paper cut. But those who served close to Erwin Rommel had to be more than pen-pushers and map-readers. In France and in North Africa Rommel did not command – he led from the front, and his presence defined the front. Hans-Joachim Schraepler was a professional officer who began his career in the Reichswehr cavalry in 1922. Rearmament and expansion under Adolf Hitler brought him to Thuringia in 1939, as adjutant to the newly organised 7th Panzer Division. Wounded in the early stages of the French campaign in 1940, he impressed Rommel sufficiently that after he recovered the general asked him to join the staff of the Afrika Korps in the spring of 1941.

Schraepler's surviving letters to his wife add significantly to our understanding of the dynamics of the desert war in its early stages. From the beginning he and the rest of Rommel's personal staff were consistently under shell fire and air bombardment. As adjutant Schraepler was responsible for replacing damaged and broken-down vehicles – no easy task in the empty desert, where even a clever staff officer could not 'organise' things from the civilian economy.

Everything had to be transported across the Mediterranean Sea, then brought forward to a constantly changing battle zone. By mid-April even Afrika Korps headquarters was living on captured British rations. That he describes them as an improvement indicates the scope of the Afrika Korps' enduring logistics problems. Fuel and water were the bare necessities. Ammunition could be rationed. Food took fourth priority.

Schraepler had been under fire before, in Poland and France. But when Rommel sent his panzers against the British fortress of Tobruk on 19 April, Schraepler was in the front line – not a usual place for of an adjutant, but virtually routine in the Afrika Korps. Like most soldiers, Schraepler tended to underplay danger when writing home. But his mention of Rommel sending him a bottle of white wine at the end of one long day is suggestive. German wine was by that time a very scarce commodity. Nor was Rommel in the habit of so handsomely acknowledging the routine good performances of members of his military family.

In general the image of Rommel's personality that emerged from these letters is of a man too busy to have much time for personalities. He was a Swabian, not a Berliner, and Swabians are not known for wearing their hearts on their sleeves. Rommel was not dour, nor was he given to venting frustration even briefly on those around him. When he did lose his temper it was with good reason, and the victim was usually a subordinate commander.

There were far worse combinations of behaviours for a CO in the close quarters and high stress of the Afrika Korps headquarters. Schraepler did so well that Rommel left him in his appointment instead of taking him along when he was promoted to command Panzergruppe Afrika in 1941. According to Schraepler, the Chief believed in periodic infusions of fresh faces in his immediate entourage. Besides, enough new officers were appearing to make an old hand doubly valuable. Rommel's replacement, Lieutenant General Ludwig Crüwell, with no experience whatever in the desert, spared no pains to let Schraepler know how pleased he was to have someone of Schraepler's experience close at hand, and how well he was regarded in Berlin. Properly interpreted, it was reasonable compensation for being left behind.

Crüwell's command style was also more than something of a relief to Schraepler. Anything but a command-post general, Crüwell used his headquarters personnel and communications equipment more than Rommel, who had been a battle captain without peer, 'a hunter, sleeping during daytime, moving at night'. Rommel had also been acting increasingly, in Schraepler's words, 'more like a head of a commando than a commanding general'. Rommel was more likely to give orders to his staff officers than to consult with them. His pattern of leaving his headquarters in the morning and returning late in the day, accepting the risks inherent in being out of touch, too often left subordinates grappling with problems in the dark. The German army emphasised command initiative at all levels. But initiative was not the same thing as unpredictability.

Despite the myths enveloping it, the Desert War was never a gladiatorial contest. North Africa was Britain's primary land theatre, usually exercising first call on weapons, supplies, and talent – a situation, paradoxically, in good part due to Rommel's developing mystique on the British side, from Churchill down. Rommel by contrast was low down on German priority lists for everything. He was making war with the Reich's pocket-change, especially as the Russian invasion in 1941 did not turn out to be the walkover High Command expected. And he recognised, better than most of his critics before and since, that his task as commander was to bridge the shortage of materiel through art and artifice.

That artifice, in passing, included taking advantage of his increasing celebrity status in Germany: the Desert Fox, idol of his men and terror of the British. Rommel enjoyed the adulation for its own sake, as one might enjoy a good steak or a single-malt scotch. But publicity also had its uses as leverage, and Rommel took pains to see that his fan mail was answered punctually.

Rommel was not in the habit of explaining himself to subordinates. He made his case separately, under four headings. First, Rommel argued, it was a mistake to assume every officer would make the most of every situation. The commander's physical presence was the best antidote to battle's 'fog and friction'. Second, the commander must keep his troops abreast of the latest tactical developments. Third, it was in the commander's own interest to have a personal perspective of conditions at the front. Success came most freely to the general whose ideas developed from the circumstances. Finally, the commander must be able to feel and think with his men. The one basic rule was to avoid artifice and posturing. The ordinary soldier has 'a surprisingly good nose' for what is true and what false.

Rommel's hands-on approach succeeded brilliantly on a small scale against enemies who reacted to it. But put larger forces into the field, give the enemy a general with the will power to stick to his own plans, and Rommel's style began to fray at the edges. And thereby hung a paradox. Rommel's style of command depended heavily on what the Germans call *Tuchfühlung* or *Fingerspitzengefühl* – a combination of situational awareness and experience-based intuition that wrote its book as it went along. To be effective it required high levels of physical, mental and emotional fitness – and those personal demands increased as the enemy improved.

Erwin Rommel was an infantryman who became a tank soldier late in his military life. Throughout his career as a foot soldier he prided himself on setting the standards for toughness and resilience wherever he went. The few weeks' fighting in France during 1940 confirmed not only his self-confidence but his confidence in himself. He saw no reason to take particular care of himself in the desert, even though he was increasingly his own best resource. But North Africa was different.

Hans-Joachim Schraepler was tough: so tough that his robust good health was regularly cited as the example that proved that Europeans over thirty could stand more than six months at a time in Africa. Like many German officers, he enjoyed criticising his Italian counterparts for what he considered their fondness for the good life. But occasionally another side emerged. Italian tents were comfortable, Schraepler mused. One could move around in them. They had canned food, tinned butter. 'The Italians have, of course, long experience in the desert. They know what one needs.'

Rommel seemed not to care. He turned 50 in 1941, and month by month his indifference saw his headquarters grow more Spartan. He would eventually spend nineteen continuous months in Africa, longer than any officer over the age of 40. He suffered from jaundice, circulation problems and digestive trouble – that last in good part a consequence of a marked indifference to food. Rommel's days in the desert were regularly fuelled by no more nourishment than a package of sandwiches, or a can of sardines and a chunk of ration bread, plus a flask of cold tea.

The rest of his physical environment was similarly austere, and has generated corresponding admiration among admirers of muddy-boots generalship. In fact Rommel's unnecessarily minimalist life style arguably did more than the objective hardships of the desert to damage his health and diminish his effectiveness.

As early as July 1941, Schraepler complained that Rommel's regular excursions to the front left him so exhausted that he was in bed by 8 p.m., and barely in shape to sign the papers put in front of him, much less consider them in detail.

Rommel's personal staff, first in the Afrika Korps and then the Panzergruppe, babied him as unobtrusively as possible, going on fishing and hunting trips to provide fresh protein, scrounging eggs and chickens, having fruits and vegetables flown in clandestinely. The Chief nevertheless endured enough spells of public weakness that in August 1942 his Chief of Staff insisted on a complete examination. The doctor, a stomach specialist from Würzburg University and Rommel's long-standing medical confidant, reported that Rommel was so debilitated by digestive trouble and low blood pressure that he was unfit to command the coming offensive. Recommended therapy amounted to a long rest. Erwin Rommel was convalescing in Germany when Montgomery and the British 8th Army launched the decisive offensive of El Alamein.

German economy in headquarters staffs has been so widely praised that it is useful to mention a counterpoint. Small numbers meant no relief. Everyone had to work long hours under high stress, and the resulting fatigue led to errors in judgment, to exaggerated personal friction, and to problems falling through cracks. All three plagued the Afrika Korps and the higher Panzer formations throughout the campaign. Schraepler was no exception. His letters home show the worsening effects of stress. They become increasingly, almost desperately, focused on the subject of leave – leave never approved because there was no one to take his place.

Schraepler died in an accident. On 9 December 1941 he was run over by a Mammoth, a captured British command vehicle pressed into service by the Germans at Afrika Korps HQ. A lapse of attention? A few seconds' delay in reacting? The records are silent, but perhaps fatigue and stress contributed directly to his death. In any case Hans-Joachim Schraepler is commemorated, along with 6,000 other soldiers of the Afrika Korps, in the memorial on the heights outside of Tobruk. Each name in its own way tells, like Rommel's, a story of flesh and spirit pushed beyond their limits in the name of duty.

Dennis Showalter

1

The Beginning

I did not really know my father, Hans-Joachim Schraepler, adjutant of General Erwin Rommel in the desert of North Africa.

Before World War II, he was stationed at a small traditional garrison town, Stolp in Pomerania. He would come home after a long day with his regiment and play with my elder brother Friedrich-Karl and me, aged four. He would not play with us for long, but it seemed to me to be intense.

In the early morning there was no time. We were still asleep when he left the house to take up his duty in his regiment. He came home at noon if there was no official lunch in the officers' mess, where he would have to assist as adjutant of the commanding officer of the regiment.

After the war my mother frequently spoke about their happy, first years of marriage, which our family spent in this beautiful small town in Pomerania, close to the home of her parents.

People used to refer to the lively town of Stolp as the 'Paris of the East'. Throughout the year there were numerous dinners and gatherings, balls in town and in the countryside, along with hunting in the vast surrounding forests in the autumn and winter.

Frequent dinners at home prepared with products from the countryside supplied by my grandmother completed the social life of my parents. But it was just the evening, before my parents were changing to go out, that belonged to us, and when my father played with us.

He took us by our arms, lifted us up and shot us high up in the air. It seemed to me as if I was approaching the sky, the infinite, a brief sensation. Then he caught us in his arms as if he always wanted to hold us, forever.

Screams, feeling of happiness. We felt safe, secure, supported by the infinite love that only parents can have for their children. Even today, I can remember those moments of happiness in that early nineteenth-century villa where my parents had rented the ground floor. I can still feel the pressure of the young lieutenant's – my father's – uniform buttons on my skinny child's body when I landed in his arms after a well-calculated flight up to the high ceiling of the living room.

Then I breathed it in: the scent of the cavalry barracks gushed out of his beautiful lieutenant's uniform, this so-typical mix of horse scent, cigar smoke, the fresh evening breeze of his way home.

My mother looked at the evening exercise full of confidence and a sense of happiness, even if she could not help feeling a slight restlessness when she saw us flying up into the air. But her trust in her husband's strength, in his accuracy, was finally stronger than her fear that something might happen to us.

This is actually my only real memory of my father in these peaceful times in Stolp, which, unnoticed by us children, were already overshadowed by dark, threatening clouds. This period ended for us with my father's transfer to Berlin in 1938.

I still remember more disjointed facts. They are mere fragments that can be somehow combined: images, passing moments and meetings, playing in the sandpit with the children of Lieutenant von Kleist, living in the same house, with Gabriele, in the children's room when it rained, or on the beautiful white beach in Stolpmünde in summer days, planted with pine forests and bushes, that bounded the Baltic Sea and the permanently wandering dunes.

My parents were fully integrated in the social activities in Stolp and in its rural environment, being members of quite a cheerful group of young married lieutenants. But I held to our evening exercises with my father, which for my brother and me ended the day.

Born at Beetzendorf on 13 October 1903, my father, Hans-Joachim Schraepler, joined the Reichswehr in 1922. The army had been limited by the Versailles Treaty to a total of 100,000 men. Promoted to Leutnant (2nd lieutenant) on 1 February 1927, he served with the 5th Prussian Cavalry Regiment, ultimately in Stolp.

Promoted to Oberleutnant (lieutenant) on 1 March 1930, he rose to the rank of Hauptmann (captain) on 1 May 1935.

In 1938, he was transferred to the Oberkommando des Heeres (OKH) or Army High Command: first to the inspectorate for riding and driving, then to the inspectorate for armoured troops, cavalry and army motorisation. In September 1939, he took part in the Polish campaign as commander of the 4th Company, Kavallerie Schützenregiment 7. He went on to fight in the west with the 7th Panzer Division, commanded by Rommel.

On 14 February 1941, my father, promoted meanwhile to major, was placed at the disposal of OKH and later appointed adjutant (IIa, general staff officer, personnel) on the general staff of the Deutsches Afrika Korps (DAK).

My father received posthumous promotion to Oberstleutnant (lieutenant colonel).

My father's account, based on fragments and discussions

In 1922 I joined cavalry regiment no. 5, successor of the Blücher Hussar Regiment, in garrison in Stolp in Pomerania. I had just finished school. The regiment belonged to a group of regiments, with a long tradition and an excellent reputation, whose existence was assured by the Treaty of Versailles. Prince Blücher was one of the leading commanders of the war of liberation against Napoleon.

I had decided on the cavalry. Despite the gradual transition into a modern professional army, which began to raise a number of questions of the military tradition, the cavalry and its officer corps felt more closely linked to traditional values than other armies of the service. The cavalry was the dream of my childhood which I had spent with my parents and siblings in a small German town of the Empire.

Stolp had a reputation as a pretty garrison town where a career officer could live quite comfortably. I felt attracted by the reputation of the regiment, its military quality, the excellent reputation of its members, their solid professionalism and their known loyalty to essential military principles.

I knew already that most members of the regiment had their family origins in Pomerania, in that ancient province, one of the pillars of the Prussian Kingdom. Many belonged to families of large landowners, of the bourgeoisie in towns and of those living in rural areas, but they also came from other provinces of the former kingdom.

But one element was decisive for me in choosing to join this regiment: despite the depressing end of World War I this regiment preserved Prussian military values, which resulted from a long historical evolution, with rises and declines.

And do not forget that the landscape around Stolp offered everything for manoeuvres and hunting: vast forests with magnificent trees, heathland, mysterious ponds and lakes, rivers and streams, rich with many kinds of fish, meadows and pastures, and rich game for hunting.

I had also heard how sympathetic and friendly the atmosphere in Stolp and in the countryside was, and how pleasant relations and contacts were between the regiment, which had been stationed in that garrison well over a hundred years, and the town and the countryside.

Thanks to these good and friendly relations, the unmarried officers and officer cadets were regularly invited to balls to dance with the daughters, but also to dinners, hunting and picnics. Town, countryside and regiment formed one family. This, as well as the proximity of the Baltic Sea and the chance of weekends in Danzig and Berlin, had convinced me to try to enter this regiment.

I was called up on 1 October 1922. I presented myself in the regiment office on time. A constable was ordered to accompany me to meet the regimental doctor.

I waited in the doctor's anteroom. Suddenly I heard through the half-closed door a harsh voice: 'Come in.'

I entered. I bowed politely. The doctor was sitting behind his desk. No reaction. I took off my clothes and the examination began.

'Have you been sick?'

'No, Mr regimental doctor,' I did not know how I should address him. He was smaller than me. I had been taught to look at the person speaking to me, so I bowed my head. But he did not like my polite gesture at all and he bellowed at me:

'Look straight ahead! Why do you bow your head to answer me?'

Another question: 'Were there signs of mental illness in your family?'

'No, Mr regimental doctor.'

Apparently he liked the way, I addressed him. He finally finished his examination, saying:

'You are in good health. You may go.'

I grabbed my clothes and left his office, naked, in direction of the waiting room. I dressed and returned with the constable to the regiment's office.

I knew well that the military way of speaking to people is often terse. The fact, however, that doctors addressed me in this tone surprised me. I thought that a doctor should express himself with gentle words, lots of love and delicacy. On the way back, the sympathetic constable explained to me that the doctor spoke to everyone in the regiment that way, which did not mean that he was malevolent. But he was easily irritated.

The regiment received me kindly. When I presented myself at the office, the cavalry captain welcomed me and even shook hands with me. The office clerk filled in a questionnaire with my personal details. Afterwards I accompanied the constable to the tailor's workshop, where several soldiers, about a dozen, worked, sitting legs crossed, sewing and repairing. I received my first uniform.

Duty began next morning. This year, we were twelve officer cadets, more than usual. Some of them were allowed to live in town. The landlords, often widows, pastors, schoolteachers or civil servants, all had one extremely useful function. In the morning, when leaving, they checked our uniform, just to ensure that all of buttons were closed and our general appearance was correct.

Work began at four o'clock in the morning, beginning in the stables with cleaning out the horses. The groom on duty during the night was ordered to ensure that the horses did not soil the straw. Once horse droppings appeared, he had to remove them immediately, not to collect them with a shovel, but to use his own hands so as not to hurt the horse. This was not always pleasant – they were often still very hot! The droppings had to be put into a specially prepared wooden box. During the stable cleaning the constable on duty walked in front of us in order to monitor our work. But when he turned his back and the horses started to do their business, we used our aprons to receive the droppings to avoid soiling the straw. But we were not always successful. The apron belonged to the state and it was strictly forbidden to use it for such a purpose.

The grooming of the horses was really quite complicated: seven brush and curry comb strokes on a length of one metre between the shoulder blades and the horse-tail, further strokes at the sides, on the crest, shoulders, withers, croup, haunches, flanks, stifles and a stroke on the head, and that was it. Brush and comb were then to be cleaned in the hallway. During the summer, it was not too difficult to do the seven brush strokes, and we were able to present a dusty brush to the constable afterwards. In winter, this was much more difficult. We officer cadets were not always very honest. In winter, and it happens each time when the constable turned us his back, we brushed the wall covered with lime, to show a dusty brush that we had fulfilled our duty according to given orders.

Each member of regiment had its own cleaning tools in a specially made wooden box. A lady would not have more paraphernalia in her cosmetic case for preservation of her own appearance than the cavalrymen of this regiment for his horse. According to the instructions given the shine box should contain: a comb, a brush for the entire horse, another for mane and tail, finally, a third for the hooves, a scraper, cloth for cleaning eyes and nostrils, a large scarf to wipe again the horse at the end of the cleaning process.

Afterwards the training began: riding, shooting, and lessons to teach us what a soldier should know for the defence of his country.

I had always been reluctant to walk. But I learned in the barrack yard in Stolp finally how to do it. The constable told me that hardly anyone knew at the beginning of his military service how to walk properly and that one could only learn it in the army. One day the commanding lieutenant remarked to me while practising, 'Officer Cadet, you march like a pregnant ballerina.' The remark irritated me somehow, and I decided to solve the problem.

In April winter training changed for summer training. Two months later, the captain examined us. Subject: stable work. I passed, which released me from that duty, to be replaced by theoretical teaching. The lessons took place in the officers' mess every evening. Dinner followed in the dining room.

It happened from time to time that we assisted at dinners in the officers' mess with some notables of Stolp and estate owners from the nearby countryside. In these cases, we were sitting in the immediate vicinity of our lieutenant. But these invitations had only one purpose: they wanted to see whether we had good manners, in particular, after having enjoyed several glasses of good wine.

With the exception of special permits, we were summoned to be present in our apartments in town or in the barracks at 21 hours. The fanfare sounded every evening at this hour, as also at four o'clock in the morning. The whole town could hear the signals.

Every year on 16 December, Prince Blücher's birthday, celebrations were organised in town. At ten o'clock in the morning there was a church service, followed by a parade at noon on the Stephansplatz and in the evening balls with theatrical performances. The festivities lasted until the early morning. The following day was free of duty.

During winter, an officer or a constable instructed us in horse riding. We rode for two months without stirrups. The squadron was subdivided into four sections A, B, C, D, each having fifteen cavalrymen. The less gifted riders were in group D. Some cavalry regiments rode on horses that were all the same colour. My regiment had horses of all colours, with the exception of the horses of the trumpeters. These were black. The horses were the sanctuary of the squadron. The cavalry captain or the lieutenant were personally responsible for them.

After training in winter, we expected the visit of the general and other personalities. When my group filed up before the general, I had the feeling that he doubted my capacity to ride a horse. As I passed him, I believed I heard the general say to the cavalry captain,

'Well, captain, do you have no other riders?'

'Excellency, wait and see,' he replied.

At the end the general remarked to the captain,

'You were right. This officer cadet is excellent,' and he gave me a sign that I took as a compliment.

After this visit training was pleasanter and also more interesting: exercises outside town and finally manoeuvres. Since I was an enthusiast of horses and riding, a lieutenant, a former racing rider, took care of my further training. I began to win prizes. The lieutenant preferred family life to a society life, though. He had a girlfriend, who visited him regularly, but she refused to clean his apartment.

Although our training began very early in the morning, the evenings were not always calm and relaxed: despite our fatigue, as soon as the officer on duty had closed the door behind him, it was time for us, the officer cadets, to wage 'war' on the different dormitories. One dormitory would attack another, invading and attacking a bed inside, in which someone slept, and then disappearing. Before the sleeping cadet realised it, he would find himself on the floor, with his bed's iron frame, boards, mattresses, blankets and sheets all tipped up. The counter-attack followed: water, pursuing the attackers. Finally, we were all so soggy that water dripped from our nightshirts. It was obviously difficult to avoid noise during the fighting. The officer would appear eventually and yell at us. We had to line up at the front of our dormitory in our wet night shirts for two hours!

One cloudy day in winter, after an exhausting duty, I felt a sudden desire for a change of air. I wanted to stroll in Berlin once again. I did not want to ask the cavalry captain for permission, because I had not been long enough in the regiment. But my will was stronger than my reason. One of my comrades shared my plan. Hence we decided to spend the weekend together in Berlin. Neither of us was on duty on the Saturday afternoon, but as the train from Berlin did not arrive in time on Monday morning in Stolp, we had to ask our constable for permission to begin that day's work at nine. He agreed, not without a hint of a certain smile, he had obviously guessed our plan. In order not to cause suspicion, we left the barracks in uniform. If an officer questioned us on the train, we would have told him that we wanted to visit an uncle in the countryside not far from Stolp. A suitcase contained our civilian clothes. Fortune seemed to smile upon us. No officer could be seen on the train. We arrived in Berlin around nine o'clock in the evening. In the meantime we had changed into civilian clothes. We booked into the hotel, and, chrysanthemum in buttonhole, we were ready to go out. It was already too late to go to the theatre. We decided, therefore, to dine in a good restaurant and then go dancing in an elegant nightclub that at the time was in vogue. Music – couples on the dance floor – champagne on the tables. I leaned against a pillar and watched the dancing. Suddenly I noticed behind another pillar in front of me a certain, only too well-known movement of a hand with a signet ring. This hand tried to take out of a silver cigarette case, which I also knew only too well, a cigarette. In my regiment, there was only one hand which had that movement, and that was this one. It was the hand of the cavalry captain, who, surrounded by several ladies, talked with gestures of his hands in a way that no one else could. He had probably taken the earlier train from Stolp, as we did not see him in our train. We froze; we felt ourselves go pale. But how could we leave this club without being noticed? Luckily, he only had eyes for the ladies around him. In a moment we regained our calm, which allowed us to leave the place without having been seen by him. The remaining hours of that night we spent happily in another dance club, less trendy than the first one. On the Sunday morning after an excellent lunch, we enjoyed horse racing and in the evening theatre, afterwards to the station to take the night train back to Stolp.

In 1927, I was appointed lieutenant. Signing up did not mean that I would automatically become a lieutenant of the regiment; according to regulations the officer corps of this regiment elected its future members. Even if I had excellent marks, I could only become member of the officer corps by election; a simple majority was sufficient. Under the rules the youngest lieutenant voted first. Years later I realised that even a good and solid background would not necessarily help you be accepted by the officer corps as one of them. After my election, as part of the election ritual, I had to pass in front of the sentry box wearing my new uniform. The first, the guard would present arms until the new lieutenant put a coin in the box, as he was not allowed to receive the offering in his hand. Everyone knew this ancient custom. To be on duty as guard on this day was very popular; and after the year of my appointment more and more lieutenants were elected into the officer corps. I was particularly proud and happy that the officer corps of this traditional cavalry regiment, the descendent of Blücher's Hussars, had elected me to be one of them.

Winter was the time for hunting in the countryside. For us officers and NCOs, participating in the hunts was part of our duty. Appropriate premises were offered to us by the landowners in the vicinity of Stolp who were former members of the regiment's officer corps. After the hunt coffee and cake (of course, not just that!) were offered. The return to the barracks was always quite late.

The hunt on 3 November was devoted to St Hubert, the patron of hunting. It was a big event for the society of Stolp, the landowners and the regiment. To underline the importance of this day, more people than usual had been invited. The day ended with a dinner in the officers' mess, for which uniform or evening dress was mandatory. The participants of the hunt had the right to wear small oak leaves in their buttonholes. The same ritual ensued each year. Trumpeters on their black horses rode first. Once the regiment and the other riders had left the town, they started a light trot to an estate approximately 14 miles away. For over ten years, the owners had received the riders of St Hubert's hunt. It ended with coffee and cake, followed by a glass of wine while the trumpeters played popular tunes. After two hours the participants would return to Stolp to get dressed for the dinner in the officers' mess at seven o'clock. St Hubert's hunt was unforgettable. The autumn colours of the countryside in Pomerania, the birch avenues, the fanfares and uniforms, the horses, the joy of all participants and to finish the day a delicious meal in the officers' mess. It was for all who had taken part in such a day, an extraordinary souvenir, which helped to overcome the depressing political situation after the fall of the Empire, the end of World War I and the continuing difficulties of the Republic of Weimar.

Life in Stolp, in 'Little Paris of the East', was quite chic. We were often invited into the countryside, which we enjoyed. Around five o'clock in the afternoon we would come back from the barracks. Quick change, then organise transport, in winter often a sleigh, in summer time a barouche or other vehicle to be on time in the countryside. In general, several of use were invited. One of us generally got a ride because of his relations. Each time we were invited, the host would urge us to take along with us a lady of a certain age, who was essential for a good end to the occasion. She and her husband were great friends of the regiment. They had a flower shop in Stolp. Without them there were no cotillions. They prepared small bouquets of flowers for the young ladies chosen by us, which they carried along in baskets. Each dancer had three to four bouquets. And then we danced the whole night – of course, under the watchful eyes of their mothers.

We also liked to go to the private and official dance parties in town. We loved the balls, organised by the various trade corporations. The regiment has always been represented by either a captain or a lieutenant. We often came home late, usually around two o'clock in the morning, even if we had to get up at four o'clock to be in time for duty beginning at half past five.

The regiment's members could go hunting, if they wanted, and the opportunity was offered every weekend in the vast forests of Pomerania, rich with big game. The commander gave permission without difficulty.

If you were not invited, you returned home about five o'clock in the afternoon, and changed to go to Cafe Reinhardt, the meeting place for the regiment with estate owners and town acquaintances.

Dinner was set in the officers' mess for seven o'clock. The meals were good and modest, but rich enough to help us withstand the cold months in winter time. The menus and wines at the official dinners at the officers' mess were select and discussion round the tables was always stimulating. The regiment was known for its social invitations. Rank dictated the seating order for the meals: at the head of the table sat the senior lieutenant, on his right and left the other lieutenants, followed by the cadets. I remember two lieutenants who were very strict with us. If we discussed duties or told a bad joke during dinner, as frequently happened, they would summon the aide of the officers' mess with their eyes to collect a Mark from the sinner to be used to pay for hunting events.

The apartments in town, if one preferred not to live in the barracks, were for us officers very pleasant and adapted to our needs. From the arrival of the regiment in Stolp in 1758 the entire life of this small and sympathetic town turned around it and its members. I had rented a small apartment with a small garden at an unusually low price. It had generally been rented to officers of the regiment. Even today, I think with emotion of my landlady of a certain age, the widow of a pastor. She was affectionate, generous and extremely patient. She could have been my mother. I had the impression that she thought of me rather like a son. She would ignore all my mistakes and errors, which I made quite often. I spent many very happy moments there. Friends came who were not the quietest, but the landlady had never heard any noise, when I met her as usual the next morning to apologise, once with a bouquet of flowers, at another time with a rabbit, which I had bought. Every time this beautiful soul said that she had heard nothing.

2

The Background

My father was 15 years old when the armistice in the railway wagon near the village of Rethondes, surrounded by the forest of Compiegne, was signed on 11 November 1918. It was in fact the signature of a defeat, a subject that private debate in Germany incriminated during the following years. He lived with his parents in a small town in Saxony, attended the local high school and prepared his graduation.

Did he discuss with his friends, schoolmates, teachers, parents questions of the future of Germany? Did he feel concerned with the general situation in Europe, in Germany? After graduation he decided to enter a cavalry regiment of the Reichswehr, his dream, which he pursued despite uncertainties about the future of Germany.

Did the political situation in Germany after the defeat affect him? He certainly discussed with friends and within his family the political and social changes in Germany. But did he believe that the new Republic could stabilise the domestic political situation and calm the political factions as they fought against each other in the streets, or that it could re-establish peace internally and create with the victorious powers and Germany's geographical neighbours a workable entente?

Did he consider the Republic of Weimar capable making every possible effort to re-introduce political and economic normality in Germany, the country in the middle of Europe? The consequences of the destruction of entire regions in the east of France and elsewhere during World War I and the human losses of all parties hung like dark clouds over the political climate on the Continent, which began to show effects on the world economy and the international monetary system.

After being proclaimed in 1918, the young Weimar Republic confronting anarchy, chaos, mutiny and uprising would not have easily survived its first months if paramilitary units of the Freikorps, consisting of volunteer soldiers returning from the front and others, had not put down armed attempts to establish a communist system in Germany.

They did not do it from enthusiasm for the new republic, but for Germany, shaken in its very foundations by the defeat, by strikes, hunger, civil unrest and armed insurrection, and by ceding German territory. The Treaty of Versailles felt like an imposition, presenting an additional heavy burden to the Weimar Republic and having a negative impact on the economic and domestic affairs; and this did not contribute to consolidation of the new Republic.

The victorious powers imposed a political and economic blockade on Germany that had substantially complicated the general situation in Europe. The first signs of a drastic poverty became evident in the streets of German towns. Two main concerns dominated public debate: on the one hand there was concern that, since the end of the war, the major questions remained unresolved, namely how, when there were conflicting political currents in the country alongside dramatically falling economic figures, a peaceful state could be restored, and on the other there was regret that the end of the war had not restored the pleasant living conditions of the last days of the Empire before the outbreak of war. The establishment of a Republic – not just a different system but rather an entirely new form of government for Germany – demanded that every citizen maintain an interest and commitment to this system. But the newly established Republic was imposed on the Germans in a negative environment. Germany did not win the Republic by a political battle, which would have been an honourable procedure. The Republic was the result of a depressing defeat and dispensing with the notion of monarchy, yet without giving up the mindset of monarchy. Many Germans took this view, while others viewed political trends after the end of the war as the result of conspiracy by the victorious powers against Germany.

It was, finally, Weimar that the Constituent Assembly chose to be its seat. The choice of this small town was justified not only for its cultural connections and its situation in the middle of Germany, but also from the wish not to identify with the 'military spirit of Potsdam' and to make it clear that, following the failure of the empire under the militaristic influences of the policy of Wilhelm II, this was going to be a new start for Germany. The choice of this town would furthermore showed that the Republic identified itself with the German intellectual identity: Goethe, Schiller and others had given Weimar the reputation of being at the heart of German culture around the world.

The responsible politicians of the new democracy should have noticed that the German citizenry was very far away from the democratic ideals and from being committed to democracy as a form of government as the future opened up. It was said at that time critically and mockingly that the 'new republic would be a republic without republicans'. The Republic has been accused of everything disagreeable that a defeat and a start-up of a state involves. Germany became a state in the hands of politicians, who ranged the interests of a political party above the interests of the nation and the welfare of the people without conceding a period of grace to the Republic, which it needed. In addition to the ongoing attempts by the victorious powers during the peace negotiations to humiliate Germany that can be found in the protocols, there was concomitant rising unemployment, galloping inflation and the melting away of private assets like butter in the sun; the period following the signing of the armistice was filled with political uncertainty. Lack of work and hunger caused dissension and political assassinations and coup attempts were organised by groups on the right as well of those tending to the left. Events during that period included a coup attempt against the Bavarian government (1923), in which Hitler was involved, arrested and convicted; but he was released a few months later. Those in power tried to win people's sympathy, yet by focusing too much on the constitution, they did not seem to notice threatening agitation from right and left, and their arguments found a certain resonance in the nation, even in military circles.

The humiliation of Germany, the dissolution of the empire of Austria-Hungary, the demise of the Ottoman Empire, the founding of the League of Nations, the increasing numbers of small states in Europe, did not create a stable situation, viewed geopolitically. The new European system was the result of the intention of the victorious powers to create by having many states a counterweight to the weakened Germany which in the middle of Europe still had its importance and was active.

The young Republic finally confronted this enormous problem that arose from the defeat, namely the uprisings of the extreme right, the communists and other political groupings, by creating the 'Reichswehr', (National Defence), a military force to help to put down unrest in the Weimar Republic. Under the supreme command of General Hans von Seeckt, officer of the former imperial army of Prussian tradition, the Reichswehr, composed of mainly of members of all grades of the former imperial forces, agreed to do everything they could 'to rescue the Republic'. For this the Reichswehr demanded recognition of a privileged position within the parliamentary system of the government. It did not take much time for people to realise that the Reichswehr had become a state within the state.

The Freikorps formed the basis of the Reichswehr, officially established in 1921 and limited to 100,000 men according to terms imposed by the Treaty of Versailles. During the first decade, the Reichswehr concentrated on providing stability; it was marked for its, well-planned and strict organisation as well as steadily improving its quality by stringent selection procedures. The Reichswehr, as a volunteer army with twelve years' service, could afford to accept only the best candidates. Many tried to enter, many were refused. By pursuing these policies and with a high degree of skilful management of the units, the chief of the army command, General von Seeckt, succeeded in forming this small professional army into elite troops fit to overcome the after-effects of World War I relatively quickly; thus he built up the core force of the future army. Tradition and revolution were the two poles between which the Reichswehr moved during these turbulent years of the new republic.

The 100,000-strong army allowed by Versailles Treaty had three cavalry divisions. The 5th Prussian Cavalry Regiment, successor in tradition to the Blücher Hussars, was established on 1 April 1920 with two garrisons in Stolp and Belgard in Pomerania. The Blücher Hussars had continuously garrisoned in Stolp since 1743 and thus was one of the oldest hussar garrisons of the Prussian army; all other regiments had to give up their traditional garrisons ordered by the Versailles Treaty.

The Reichswehr was, in a military sense, in a particularly difficult situation. The Treaty of Versailles had prohibited possession of any modern weapons, such as planes, tanks, heavy artillery and chemical weapons. It had become some kind of border guard and police force and was forced to accept a situation which was psychologically hard to assume, and they felt degraded. Further provisions of the Versailles Treaty deepened this feeling: their presence was limited to only a part of the former German Reich; there were measures to prevent their maintaining or constructing fortifications on the left bank of the Rhine, as well as on the right bank; there were restrictions on the assembly of troops as well as on all military exercises of all kinds and on the maintenance of any substantive arrangements for a mobilisation in those areas. An international Control Commission (CMIT) under the direction of the French General Nollet was charged with monitoring the disarmament of Germany (up to 1927) and to neutralise the arms industry, including companies such as Krupp. International commissions monitored shipping on Rhine, Elbe, Oder and Danube.

The disarmament was psychologically and sentimentally accepted neither by the officer corps nor by the German people. But the election of Hindenburg, a monarchist and respected personality, seemed to calm down the internal situation and consolidate it. Parallel to it, the economic perspectives in connection with some foreign political successes began to improve. Life became again pleasant, in this 'imperial' Republic, as it was often formulated.

The persistent discussions on possible modifications of the Constitution ended rather abruptly at the moment of the world economic crisis. The government saw an opportunity to exploit the crisis to cancel the reparations imposed by the Treaty of Versailles. It dissolved the Parliament in 1930. But the election results from 1932 jolted everyone inside and outside Germany. Hitler's National Socialists won 18 per cent, representing six million votes, and this gave them 107 seats in the Reichstag. The debates about the possible reintroduction of the monarchy became more intense. A new phase began in Germany, which nobody had expected.

Four reasons prompted the vote for the National Socialists: first, the world economic crisis was causing general impoverishment; second, there was lack of unity and weak strategy in the left wing parties; third, rising nationalist feelings were fed by the complex caused by having lost the war, and the refusal of former members of the armed forces of the Empire to accept what had happened at the end of World War I; and finally there was the charismatic personality of Hitler.

A significant majority of Germans were already hoping for a strong personality to be at the head of the republic as early as 1918 and 1919: someone who would show a strong will and wield the authority to solve problems. They wanted someone who would be authoritarian but who could somehow identify with the idea of monarchy.

The Reichswehr, called the Wehrmacht after 1935, initially kept their usual reserve. But Hitler was busy pursuing his objectives. The political importance of the armed forces came above all from support from Hitler and his party: they in their turn needed the military for the execution of their plans. The Wehrmacht, exposed to these different currents and still feeling the virus of revenge, if not subject to it, had the illusion that they dominated Hitler and his troupe politically, or at least imagined they were in a position to do so.

At that period there were three representatives of the military tradition in command: General von Blomberg, Minister of War, General von Fritsch, chief of the General Staff of the Army, and General Beck, chief of the General Staff. They were utterly wrong, and this would have, for Germany, Europe and the world, terrible consequences. They did not see that Hitler, a simple soldier in World War I, was nursing a deep mistrust towards those who had failed to avoid defeat.

If a resistance movement had been formed at that time, and had actually acted, there was no real chance that there would have been any popular support for it. Yet – leaving aside the thousands of Germans who in those years did not see any other way than emigration – resistance was organised after the unconstitutional seizure of power by Hitler. There was a feeling that state authority in its entirety should not fall in the hands of the Nazis. Secret meetings were organised, initially attended mainly by socialists and communists as well as by members of the two churches; long before the beginning of World War II members of the bourgeoisie, civil servants and members of the officer corps were involved. Committed to swear allegiance to the person of Hitler the soldiers of the Reichswehr/Wehrmacht, trained with Prussian values, were prisoners of a deep dilemma, with which a large number could only live with difficulty. The profession of soldier called, according to tradition, for apolitical and neutral behaviour and loyalty to the head of state, which would explain why honour and obedience always played a special role in the Reichswehr and later in the Wehrmacht. Both terms were inexorably linked by the military connotations.

But a change came on 30 January 1933, the day of the *Machtergreifung* (seizure of power) by Hitler. The, until 1937, direct intervention of the Führer and Chancellor in military questions does not seem to have taken place. But Hitler did not forget the Reichswehr. On the day of President Paul von Hindenburg's death, 2 August 1934, the troops, on instruction of the Minister of War, Werner von Blomberg, were sworn to Adolf Hitler:

> I swear by God this sacred oath that I shall render unconditional obedience to Adolf Hitler, the Führer of the German Reich and people, supreme commander of the armed forces, and that I shall at all times be ready, as a brave soldier, to give my life for this oath.

The Weimar Republic had provided for the first time in German history that the soldier should swear his oath of allegiance not to a person but to the constitution; but with this oath the personal bond, this time to the Führer, once again became the institution. On 4 February 1938 personnel and structural changes at the Wehrmacht followed. The High Command of the army was formed, and Hitler secured his direct influence on the entire armed forces.

Since the autumn of 1934 it had been clear what was happening, but it was on 16 March 1935 that the government in Berlin announced the development of the German Wehrmacht, which extended to twelve army corps with thirty-six divisions. On 21 May 1935, the government introduced the general conscription for men over eighteen years of age.

***

Up to the end of her life, affected by the national and international consequences of the last war, my mother had rarely spoken with me about this era and the efforts of the Republic of Weimar to position itself both nationally and internationally. Likewise she mentioned very rarely the position of her husband, my father, in regard to these historic developments.

She only mentioned that it had been his wish, after school, to become an officer and to serve in a cavalry regiment. I had the impression in these conversations, that my parents were deeply entrenched in notions of 'everyone for himself', each in his own system: my mother in the countryside dominated by the prevailing ideas of large landowners in Pomerania, my father in the ideas of a Reichswehr which did not identify itself with the Weimar Republic.

The policies and plans of the Republic, which existed outside their beliefs and conceptions of life and their personal engagement, did not seem to interest them particularly. But neither the one nor the other felt in any way attracted by the theories and methods of the author of the book *Mein Kampf*. His letters from North Africa, addressed to my mother, indicate this quite clearly. This impression has been confirmed many times in my conversations with her after the war, after we had left the former Soviet Occupied Zone, and had finally settled in Bonn. She said that, with the exception of a few people, their friends inside and outside the regiment in Stolp, and the friends and neighbours of her parents in Pomerania, all felt emotionally and politically distant from the Nazi troops in party uniform who presented their medals and awards provokingly and exercised their power brutally. In one of these discussions she mentioned also that General Rommel would not have officially requested the High Command of the Wehrmacht in Berlin to transfer her husband to North Africa, if he had thought that he was close to the ideas of the Nazis.

Years after the war, one day, I asked my mother:

'What did your parents say about the pursuit of the Jews and the discrimination against them? Did they believe that it was best not to talk about it?'

She replied:

The Jews lived in Poland, beyond the border. We had heard some very vague rumours about certain programs, that the Poles were pursuing them.

Your grandparents lived in the countryside. They led a life that was actually far from the events happening outside of their region. At the centre of their activities and interests was, of course, the management of the property with the given resources in an economically difficult time, the family and the neighbours. They all belonged to the same milieu.

And the officers corps, you have to understand, still somehow thought that nothing had changed in military values since the nineteenth century. Young girls had to obey their parents, which created often difficulties for me in my generally solid and affectionate relationship with my parents. When your father felt that he loved me and wanted to marry me, my parents were horrified.

He did not come from our region in Pomerania or from the countryside. They separated us. We waited one year and wrote each other many letters. Your grandparents agreed finally.

To resume, we knew of course that the Russia of Lenin and Stalin was communist. We also knew that the Jews had a different religion from us, and lived in the towns and cities. They were bankers, professors, scientists and doctors, like our physician Dr Kaufmann, who had always examined you. He was a very cultured person and highly esteemed by my parents and neighbours. When the Soviet army attacked our region in 1945, he committed suicide. The Jews were intellectuals. We lived in the countryside, in our system. We did not know them, we met rarely.

3

Dusk

World War II started in a phase of my life when I was beginning to look around me and take notice of what was going on. I did not know, of course, the reasons why Hitler ordered the Wehrmacht, after the signing the German-Soviet Non-Aggression Pact, to attack Poland on 1 September 1939 mentioning Polish provocations, nor why England, followed by France, declared war on Germany on two days later, following on from the provisions of the English statement 31 March 1939 guaranteeing independence for Poland; nor did I understand why later, in 1941, Hitler had attacked the Soviet Union, although he had signed a non-aggression pact with Stalin.

The war simply began. Mobilisation. The last days before the decampment to Poland passed in the usual atmosphere of a mobilisation. Technically, it was just a replay of when my father prepared to leave on manoeuvres. But this time, it was different. War was imminent. It was above all the uncertainty of the outcome and the return of my mother's husband, our father, that dominated the preparations. There were mixed feelings. War meant for my mother, she told me later, when we recalled those days, that the policy had been a failure.

My father's aides came: he cleaned his weapons, boots and shoes. Recruits took his tightly packed luggage away. He made some telephone calls to his father, his sister and parents-in-law, and, finally, next morning bade farewell to my mother, tapping me on the head – then he was gone. The war had begun for us. Silence spread in the apartment. My mother tried to hide her feelings before us. The war began to weigh on her. Many years later, she told me that she had accepted that her husband had a military career, and also that he would go to war one day. But this war against Poland harassed her. The international situation had become too complex. She could see no solutions. I noticed furtive tears.

After the war against Poland, I saw my father for a while, but then the war against France began. He became a member of the general staff of the 7th Panzer Division commanded by Rommel, colonel at that time.

As later in North Africa, he wrote to his wife every day. My mother preserved the letters. When the bomb attacks on German towns stepped up and the living quarters in Gera were not spared, she brought her husband's letters written in Poland and in France to her parents in Pomerania. She only kept with her the letters sent from North Africa. The other letters got lost when the Soviet army occupied Pomerania.

France capitulated after six weeks. On 5 June Rommel crossed the Somme. By the 7th he had reached the suburbs of Rouen and on the 10th the English Channel, close to Dieppe. The success of the 7th Panzer Division was to a large extent due to the speed and the technical superiority of their tanks. Rommel proved to be an excellent strategist and tactician, knowing how to use all the means at his disposal to mobilise his troops.

This success, the result of Rommel's strategic talents, his brilliance, his personal commitment and the speed of his division was perhaps one of the reasons for the difficulties with the High Command of the army that he would have when commanding the Afrika Korps. His military successes and his relationship with Hitler during this phase of the war caused envy among some generals; but they also they made of him one of the most famous generals of World War II.

After signing of the ceasefire agreement on 25 June 1940 in Compiègne, the General Staff of 7th Armoured Division remained in France. In the following months, my father accompanied Rommel on various official visits.

What were the reasons for this war against Poland, against France? Much later, and only from comments my mother made, I learned that my father had questioned the political reasons for starting World War II in 1939, which by 1940–41 was understood to be only just beginning, and wondered why the efforts for peace had not been pursued before the war.

***

After the ceasefire of June 1940 and before the German attack on the Soviet Union in June 1941, the supreme command of the army were examining ways to hit British interests. Great Britain was a world power and her colonial holdings around the world made her the dreaded enemy of Germany.

The control of North Africa, Egypt and the Near East was a classic problem of European history. Napoleon had already tried to tackle this question but it brought him no military glory, and it appeared again as a factor in the Turkish–German alliance of 1914. It was material also in the discussions held in Berlin at the end of 1940 and the beginning 1941, in which the navy and air force proposed action against the maritime routes of the United Kingdom. Although the way around the Cape of Good Hope is longer and relatively safe, Britain relied heavily on the main route to the Indian Ocean that passed from the Mediterranean and through the Suez Canal and the Red Sea.

This way was shorter, but more vulnerable. The strategists of the Third Reich fully understood that this route through the Mediterranean was one of the pillars of British interests. British military bases on islands in the Mediterranean, such as Malta, protected the shipping route between Gibraltar and Egypt. After examining all details, the High Command of the Wehrmacht in Berlin suggested landing troops in North Africa near the Moroccan border and advancing towards Egypt, while trying to occupy the strategically important islands of Malta, Crete and Cyprus, with an eye ultimately on Asia Minor, Turkey and Iraq. Further strategic goals would be to make use of oil resources in the Middle East and to hit British interests in and around the Indian Ocean, with a view to encircling the Soviet Union from the south.

There was another area that played a not unimportant role in the deliberations of the supreme command of the Wehrmacht. The ports of West Africa, part of the French colonial possessions, could be transformed into submarine bases in case of a submarine war. This would have special importance in planning for preventative measures against a possible intervention by the United States, which was already in prospect at this time.

The implementation of this plan would have required the participation of Spain, but Franco refused. So while most German troops were involved in preparations for a possible invasion of England, perhaps even at this stage in preparations for war against the Soviet Union, Italy became the main ally for war in and around the Mediterranean.

Since the beginning of the deliberations for action against British interests in and around the Mediterranean the shadow of an attack against the Soviet Union hung over the project. As usual, when Hitler had signed the non-aggression pact with the Soviet Union on 23 August 1939 it was with the intention of playing for time and to isolate the Soviet Union internationally and politically. Did Stalin suspect Hitler's intention? He had signed a secret protocol on the division of Poland as an amendment to the non-aggression pact. Contrary to the warnings of some German generals regarding the danger of an attack against the Soviet Union, Hitler decided to open a second war front. The German Wehrmacht crossed the border and attacked the Soviet Union on 22 June 1941. The war in the East did not end before winter 1941, as Hitler had speculated. Clouds piled up over Germany.

My father's letters from North Africa were clear about this point written in the second half of 1941. He was clear in his criticism and pessimistic regarding the war, if could not be terminated before winter of 1941. He feared serious disadvantages for the Afrika Korps in Libya, for the prospects of its mission. But above all he feared a prolongation of the war and the entry of the United States.

The signs of German success in North Africa were weak from the very beginning even aside from the distractions of the war against the Soviet Union. The Italian army did not have either strategically or militarily a good reputation. British troops had pushed it out of the Italian colony of Somalia and were approaching Tripoli. In addition, the squadrons of the Royal Air Force stationed in Gibraltar, Malta and Alexandria dominated the Italian fleet in the Mediterranean; this had suffered heavy losses in November 1940 and at the beginning of 1941 and considered itself no longer in a position to attack the British fleet successfully in the Mediterranean. Securing supply-lines for the Afrika Korps became therefore the persistent concern of my father and was one of the most difficult issues for Rommel in this campaign, which ended with the German surrender in North Africa about two years later.

***

When Hitler decided to send troops to North Africa, he nominated Rommel supreme commander. He in turn asked my father to become a member of his staff. My father wrote:

Still in France, 9 February 1941

. . .

This morning Rommel called from Wiener Neustadt. He has been promoted lieutenant general. He did not speak about his future mission. I guess Libya. Hopefully he will not arrive too late, since the Italians are flinching under British pressure. Rommel has asked the personnel administration to transfer me to his staff and expects me to come. He will certainly command a corps.

In any event, he will be leaving Berlin, where he is having discussions, during the next few days. I shall hear more from him pretty soon.

I have to hurry now, to write my letter to Rommel.

The campaign in North Africa was charged from the very outset with questions about the strategic and political consequences: was Italy in a position to secure the supply of the Afrika Korps and its own troops by sea between Italy and North Africa in the long term, and could Germany cope with two war fronts?

4

The Context of the Letters

From his arrival in Tripoli my father wrote daily to my mother, or at least he tried to do so. It depended on the situation at the front and Rommel's front inspections, in which he frequently took part. He described in detail the difficult beginnings of the Afrika Korps, including the installation of an infrastructure from Tripoli to supply the rapidly advancing force on a continent in nothing comparable with the European and on which the Wehrmacht had not yet collected experience.

Already in his first letters my father indicated a problem, which would not leave the German troops until their capitulation two years later: the establishment and maintenance of an infrastructure that would constantly change yet was required to supply troops in rough and sparsely populated desert terrain with road conditions for which the vehicles coming from Germany were technically unfit. Wear and tear on the vehicles had con-sequences for supply to the troops on the journeys from the ports – always supposing, that is, that the supply vessels arrived unnoticed and unmolested by the Royal Navy and the Royal Air Force into Tripoli and other ports.

The mission assigned to Rommel and his Afrika Korps on the African continent was difficult. Germany was supposed to help his Italian ally in a region outside of Europe, where up to now it had had neither natural nor historical interests, nor was it anchored by other links. In contrast to Mussolini's position which was mainly motivated by domestic reasons, Hitler's decision for a deployment on the African continent was motivated to launch a blow against the global interests of London on one of its main sea routes, hoping, if possible, even to cut it. The choice of the Mediterranean for German military operations was obvious; after having passed through the Straits of Gibraltar British ships had to cross the Mediterranean to get to the narrow Suez Canal and the Red Sea, the shortest route to the Indian Ocean and their colonies.

My father wrote long letters to my mother. Many were drafted early in the morning before the fighting started, some after midnight, often only after the Royal Air Force had unloaded their bombs, when he found himself back in his office, often covered with rubble, dust and splinters. In the second half of 1941, the staff of the Afrika Korps was exposed to intensive bombing, which considerably aggravated working conditions.

For my father the times which he would reserve for his dialogue with my mother varied. If British bombing hindered his writing in the evening, he calmly finished his letter next morning, sometimes after bombing, sometimes even as the last bombs fell nearby. When the Royal Air Force began to unload their bombs on the site of the staff as well during the second half of 1941, apparently wanting to hit Rommel personally, my father could not help but expressing his admiration for the successful work of the British secret service, criticising at the same time the inefficiency of the German secret service and complaining in one of his last letters that it often left the Panzergruppe Afrika without information about the intentions of the enemy. Hence they were in no way informed, as my father wrote, about the British preparations for the counter-offensive Operation Crusader with hundreds of tanks in November 1941, which surprised Rommel and forced him to retreat.

The censors of the German security services in Munich rarely blackened his letters. To avoid any complaints in potential disciplinary procedures against him subsequently, he remarked from time to time with his sense of humour that he avoided talking about politics with comrades and other visitors, including officials from the ministries or from the foreign office. In reality, his letters were bursting with reports of his political discussions, the contents of which he hid among letters consisting of several pages written for eyes of third persons in a tiring hand. As division adjutant of the staff of the Afrika Korps, he easily found opportunities to send letters to Germany by trusting people travelling to Germany on a mission, on leave or discovering other ways to dispatch his letters avoiding the field post controlled by the censors in Munich.

To his wife he mentioned everything he saw, said and felt, and described with whom he had spoken about concerned him and how he assessed the changing situation of the war front. He described his life in a way that, as I read his letters, I felt present in this constant dialogue between my parents.

It became clear that he needed this exchange with my mother, in addition to his talks with comrades in his tent or elsewhere, accompanied by a good glass of Scotch whisky captured from the British – the first he had tasted – or a cup of coffee or a bottle of wine. The discussions were always conducted with certain precautionary measures to prevent the German secret service, which was active on the African front as everywhere, reporting on it to Berlin.

But the urge was strong in him to tell to someone everything that worried him, what he thought and what oppressed him, though he knew that the control of letters by German censorship endangered him as all others when he was obliged, because of a lack of other opportunities, to entrust his letters to the field post. Overall, my mother received several hundred closely written pages.

The letters were a continual dialogue between two people, in which a third could only penetrate with difficulty. My mother, therefore, was always kept informed about his state of mind, of all his concerns about the course of the war in North Africa. These intensified after the attack on the Soviet Union in June 1941, but, apart from noting the gloomy prospects of this front, that it would not finish before winter began, he never slipped into any kind of moaning, but he clearly felt that the mission of the Afrika Korps (from August 1941 part of Panzergruppe Afrika) was in the end just a cog in the war strategy of Berlin.

The letters written during the second half of 1941 expressed his concern about the growing burden for Germany caused by the international situation, which increased after the attack of the Soviet Union. He wondered how far Germany could stand the pressures of war and about the possible situation if the war ended one day.

He soon became aware of the political and strategic weakness of the German front in North Africa, confronted at the end of 1941 by a well-supplied British army, but also of the weakness of the front in the Soviet Union, if the war would did not end by winter. These were all issues that the censors would have viewed as subversion to be followed by harsh disciplinary consequences and penalties if the letters fell into their hands.

Their unique historical value results from the fact that only very few members of the Afrika Korps had such a close and comprehensive overview on the first phases of the war in Libya as my father, as a member of the staff of the Afrika Korps placed between staff and fighting troops. Visitors coming from Germany or from the front went first to see him to get information and to pass information before meeting Rommel or others – they always well supplied with drinks.

This war, hardly known in Germany, took place under extremely difficult conditions, comparable to no other front, he used to say in his letters: unbearable heat during the day, often at night cold temperatures, sandstorms, diseases, continual bombing by the Royal Air Force, lack of shelter in the desert and constant deficiencies in supplies.

It often happened that the censorship department sent back letters written by members of the Afrika Korps or of the other divisions with instructions to proceed against their drafters, if they expressed critical impressions of the war in North Africa and its severity, sometimes written in the aftermath of a harsh battle on African soil. These documents were to be presented to Rommel, but passed first to my father. He sometimes informed my mother about these cases, as a warning to himself that, in fact, he never respected himself.

His letters reflect the different phases of the deployment of the Afrika Korps, a few months after its arrival becoming a member of the newly established Panzergruppe Afrika. They present at the beginning of 1941 when he arrived a young officer full of confidence in the strategy of Berlin after signature of the German-Soviet Non-Aggression Pact (1939) and the quick successes against Poland and France, but his attitude changed in the course of the year. He became critical, was sometimes discouraged.

He like many others had initially assumed that the deployment in northern Africa would only be a short interval, followed by peace. The withdrawal of British troops from the Cyrenaica after the arrival of the Afrika Korps and the fast advance of the front to the Egyptian border – my father was already imagining private visits in Cairo – seemed to confirm this analysis. But soon after his arrival in Tripoli he mentioned to his wife that the poor quality of the equipment sent from Germany to Tripoli was worrying him. The Afrika Korps would pay for it one day. But my father was an officer and had to fulfil his duty. His close relationship with Rommel, whose personality and tireless dedication to the mission stimulated him anew repeatedly. This includes his admiration for the particular style of Rommel's contacts with the troops, which he always mentioned in his letters with admiration, although he criticised Rommel's frequent presence on the front line because of the risk.

His letters did not conceal his criticism, when read closely, of the enormity of Berlin's strategy to attack British interests by a campaign on a continent which effectively was unknown to Germany. They indicate doubts on the reliability of the political stance in Berlin to the front in North Africa, which resulted in considerable human losses by death, wounds and illness and by psychological problems.

Some months after the attack on the Soviet Union in June 1941, his views in the letters became clearer. For my father the attack was a sign that the priorities in the strategic vision of Hitler had changed and the front in North Africa had moved down to second place on the list of priorities, which caused tactical and strategic disadvantages for the Afrika Korps/ Panzergruppe Afrika that ultimately produced a negative outcome: reduced supplies of soldiers, ammunition, weapons, means of transport and so on, and attendance of the air force only sporadically. The effects of the British bombardment and the sinking of German and Italian ships between Italy and

North Africa transporting supplies went so far that soldiers gave up their hopes of leave if they could not leave Africa by air.

The special desire of my parents to write every day was intended to make the geographical distance between them and the time intervals between their letters seem unimportant. This idea helped them to accept their separation as something that, though inevitable, would preserve their mutual closeness.

Their intention was to adapt to the new separation, the third since their marriage in 1931, and to fill it as far as they could with long letters, full of discussions, exchanges and reflections. In fact every one of their words expressed their wish to come together as soon as the circumstances permitted it. This approach filled my father's letters with a wealth of information about the war, the Afrika Korps, General Rommel, the morale of the troops, the value of the British army, the British motivation to defend an empire, the difficulties of living in a different climate, the specific nature of a war on another continent and the depressing prospects opened up by the war launched in 1939. To keep track of their letters, they numbered them.

My mother's letters to my father were lost during the retreat of the Afrika Korps under British pressure in November and December 1941. My father's car was captured as his aide was driving wounded comrades to the field doctor. But, from odd comments of my father on matters raised by my mother, it can be assumed that she also kept him closely informed about living in Germany during the 1941 as the population felt the impact of the war starting to hit.

My father's letters amazed me, not only because it was my father and I was starting to get to know him by reading them, but I was also surprised also by my parents' determination to create a lively and strong link between them to get over the separation that they basically accepted. The letters were conceived as an ongoing conversation, and they were intended to contain every detail of every day that they passed without each other.

The contents of my father's letters changed from purely personal issues to technical comments, reports and comments on the situation at the front, reproducing discussions and describing his efforts to create a personal environment that facilitated contacts and fostered personal atmosphere in the desert.

They revealed at the same time my father's desire, despite increasingly negative signs regarding the course of the war, to keep up with his hope for peace, a position that he could preserve only with great effort, being under special British pressure from November 1941, suffering his own losses and the lack of supplies that forced Rommel to retreat. Words such as 'victory' were not there any more in his last letters, although he referred repeatedly to the strategic successes of the Afrika Korps and Panzergruppe Afrika under Rommel's command, but his hopes for peace, for an end of the war, diminished. He did not avoid mentioning, in this context, Rommel's unsuccessful attempts to occupy Tobruk, fortified by the British with technical sophistication and skill.

He described encounters and battles, analysed them and forwarded questions regarding the benefits of German action and its impact on the enemy. But also, in detail and with much personal pleasure, he described his dinner parties with his comrades and the menus – the ingredients of which often came from British spoils – and their efforts to create a familiar environment around them. These were evenings, which took their minds off the war in the desert. He mentioned as well, of course, the opulence of the menus in the Italian mess, the descriptions of which were full of both criticism and irony.

Some of his decryptions were also about excursions to hunt gazelle in the stony desert and swimming in the sea to refresh mind and body. But he also described illnesses, his own and others', and the army of flies and biting sand fleas that attacked the soldiers, causing their wounds to suppurate, and the dangers of venomous snakes, and, of course, the daily heat, followed at certain seasons by cold nights, and finally the terrible siroccos which blew sand and dust into every corner of their tents, their offices and their belongings.

He mentioned just about everything: what he noticed, what he felt, what he did, and, of course, he spoke also about his excursions with Rommel and the pleasant moments he and his comrades spent together from time to time, because his well-organised aide always prepared something special to eat despite the rudimentary equipment, and they organised something to drink: wine, whisky or coffee – a large part of it came from British stocks.

Then, of course, relaxed, discussion started about the war, Rommel's strategy, the constant problems of supply and Berlin politics, with certain reserves. Comments on the speeches of the Führer were avoided for obvious reasons. But they thought also of Germany – their beautiful Germany, the mounting difficulties, their families – and they wondered how all this will turn out in the end.

His letters offer a very lively and rare insight into that area between the front and the staff of the Afrika Korps during the Libya–Egypt campaign, about the difficulties of every day life in the desert, the organisation of supplies from Germany to the front and the changing approach to their objectives, initially presented as easily to fulfil, but already during the second half of 1941 proving rather challenging.

On the state of mind of the German troops, moving between hope, confidence and reality, my father's letters are a rich of source showing the problems of imposing the war plan on the fighting troops in a positive way in order to persuade them to continue.

They do not hide that after the beginning of the offensive against the Soviet Union my father began to doubt the chances of success for the mission of the Afrika Korps that were accentuated by the retreat in November and December 1941 under British pressure, although at the time the tragedy of Stalingrad (19 November 1942–2 February 1943) with its dramatic impact on the German population as a sign of the possibility of German defeat in the war overall could not have been foreseen.

Not surprisingly, the letters also describe how Rommel's strategy on the continent were determined by the given objectives of Berlin and the climatically and politically different conditions compared to the previous campaigns against Poland and France. My father observed, summarised, developed his own ideas and related his impressions often to the last detail to my mother, as well as providing at the same time information about his own military career in the Reichswehr.

His letters were moving as my father gained more and more the impression that the objectives of the North Africa front – to break British interests in the Mediterranean – were beginning to disappear far into the distance when confronted to British superiority in air, on land and at sea even as Germany was extending or creating new theatres of war.

His dreams and hopes of visiting Cairo one day or to spend Christmas 1941 with his family in Gera finally vanished.

***

There are clear signs that he thought Germany was over-reaching itself when Berlin's policies led to international confrontation. He suffered as an officer in that evolution. His last letter written in December does not reveal clearly whether he had learned about the American declaration of war on Japan on 8 December 1941 after its attack on Pearl Harbor, one day before his death. In several letters he revealed that he was worried about the political position of the United States.

My father's writing style was precise, clear and frank, as if he wanted to share his worries about the development of this war with someone in his confidence. This was, of course, my mother. His letters reveal a balanced analysis, but, despite significant negative comments on the evolution of the war, most of the time his optimism and patriotism, worthy of a cavalry officer, were dominated, corresponding to his character. His letters show the typical restraint of a person who had embraced the military career as a vocation at a difficult period in Germany, after World War I and at the beginning of the Weimar Republic. The Reichswehr followed a policy of restraint with regard to the unrest and political problems in the young Republic after the controversial negotiations of the Versailles Treaty that weighed heavily on the history of Europe. This background, and innate caution, probably encouraged my father, aware as he was of the omnipresence of censorship and the monitoring of the secret service around them in Africa, to avoid discussing sensitive issues in his letters so as not to be accused before a court martial – though his letters offer enough grounds for censoring when the guidelines became more and more severe, as he mentioned in one of the letters.

Political reserve did not mean for him, however, disinterest, nor that he had no opinion on political and military developments. But the years in the Reichswehr certainly helped him to choose words that respected the censors, in case they were read, and were understandable only to those for whom the letters were intended.

The great majority of the letters were written under the varying pressures of war, resulting from the geopolitical and strategic position of the Afrika Korps on one hand and of Great Britain on the other. But while British troops were defending and making secure the worldwide interests of Great Britain, the German presence in North Africa depended for its position in the list of military objectives only on the political will of the Führer in Berlin. This difference in motivation and political interests ultimately coloured military confrontation between the two countries in North Africa and finally favoured Great Britain.

**

A military career corresponded with my father's professional inclinations. He accepted war as action against an enemy, defined as such by the political leadership of a country. This was part of the military tradition as he viewed it. But he noticed in Africa that war can have different facets and that the war on this continent was the result of a Berlin-born conception of war that was forever changing. It neither corresponded to the traditional ideas of an officer of the former Reichswehr nor did it really represent German interests, or the vision of a war according to classical European models. It was a long way off from the way even World War I had developed, with its harrowing legacy of fields of white graves with the crosses of many nations in France and other parts of Europe.

The Panzergruppe Afrika was obliged in the course of war to adapt to new geographical realities: the desert was an overwhelming force, a challenging mass of sand and dust with extremely unpleasant climatic conditions, made worse by the lack of supplies, of green vegetation and of water. Such conditions were difficult enough for the troops to bear but the special features of Berlin warfare weighed heavy on top of everything else. The unsuitability of German equipment for use in the desert, of the vehicles particularly, was one of the features that my father used to use as barometer of the political attitude of Berlin to the front in North Africa.

Yet there are no critical comments on the quality of the tanks to be found in his letters, occupying as they did a key element in the advance in the direction of Egypt. In contrast, though, was his permanent concern for the replenishment of supplies for the German and Italian troops across the Mediterranean. Mussolini had taken this important role, but despite repeated complaints never fulfilled it to Rommel's satisfaction. Furthermore, British superiority in the Mediterranean was never questioned, either by Italy or Germany.

The situation in Germany at times of war and its impact on the daily lives of the population as it was confronted by the first waves of bombing on towns and by increased calls for sacrifice by the Nazi leadership after beginning of the Russian offensive all served to influence the morale of the fighting troops in North Africa. My father did not hide his concern in his letters that he was worried when he thought about the future of Germany. For him, conscious of his position as German officer, the war in North Africa was a lost war, a war without future.

Despite the military superiority of Great Britain during the second half of 1941, German troops did have some impressive successes, thanks to the operational capacity of the Panzers, the strategic competence of General Rommel and the fighting spirit of the commanding officers and soldiers – despite serious losses, the harsh climate, poor health, shortage of ammunition and vehicles, and the lack of fuel, water and healthy food.

The courage of German troops in the desert did not exclude moments of painful reactions of dismay and even disgust of this war affecting even commanding officers risking disciplinary procedures.

Positive speculation, expressions of hope and restrained observations merged into a mixture of reflection, analysis, sentiments and wishes that this war, which he did not want in his heart, would soon come to an end so that he could take up again his old life with his family, his friends, and his comrades, though he understood it would not be the same.

His hopes for an imminent end to the war were coupled with various hints about his home leave: perhaps he would celebrate Christmas 1941 with his family, or if not then maybe in January, but surely no later than summer of

1942. But it became clear that the leaders of the Panzergruppe Afrika, and in particular the commander of the Afrika Korps, General Crüwell, did not want to let him go because he was, besides Rommel, the only remaining officer having taken part since the beginning of this campaign, generally reputed as the adjutant with irreplaceable experience.

Rommel's thrust in spring benefited above all from the fact that his opponent, General Wavell, had been requested to send some of his troops to other regions of the Mediterranean, first to Greece, then to Syria and into Iraq to deal with situations critical for British interests. This circumstance favoured the fast Italian-German advance to the Egyptian border in March 1941 and facilitated the beginning of the blockade of Tobruk with its strategically important port which, occupied once by German troops, was supposed to become the principal harbour to supply troops.

The war in North Africa after the inglorious withdrawal of the Italian troops leaving significant quantities of war materials and other goods behind them, on which my father commented in one of his letters, was at the end solely dependent on Rommel's personality, his talent for strategy, his personal commitment and his ability, despite adverse and harsh living conditions and other difficulties, to fill the troops with enthusiasm.

After the attack of the Soviet Union in June 1941 the mood in Germany changed gradually owing to the pain of loss in families and the effects of bombing as well as the serious losses in North Africa. Among groups of friends questions about the future of Germany came up, a topic that my father mentioned repeatedly in his letters. But he did not know that the year after his death would see the turn of this war that ended three years later, on 8 May 1945, with the collapse of Germany.

5

The Adjutant's Letters
20 February–19 April 1941

Rome, 20 February 1941 (postcard)
Dearest,
My first greetings since my departure. Overnight in Rome. We arrived at around 1.00 a.m. The trip with General Streich passed as planned and it was interesting. Nobody knew anything about our presence in Libya. Only on arriving in Rome did we learn that Karl [code name for Rommel] had asked by telegram for the immediate arrival of General Streich in Tunis. So we shall fly to Karl straightaway at lunchtime today. Until then I have some time and will have look around Rome in the rain.

Rome, 20 February 1941
Dearest,
This morning I wrote my first card to you in a hurry. Streich went to meet the military attaché von Rintelen. I am, of course, rather curious to know more about our deployment. But I'll have the necessary information at the latest tonight in Tunis, if we can fly. It is still questionable; it has been raining since the early morning . . .

I walked around the centre of Rome in the rain; it was enough for the time being. I have seen the giant buildings of the war ministry and other ministries. Of course, you find remnants of ancient Rome everywhere, archways, walls, many fountains. If I did not know that I would come here again, I would, despite the rain, have rented a cab so as to have a look around the town. But on the way back from Africa, I will have the regular stop-over in Rome, hopefully then without rain.

Tripoli, 21 February 1941
Dearest, I announce my arrival in Tripoli.
From the plane we noticed a German convoy on the Mediterranean, also

several planes of the German Air Force, torpedo boats, then the coasts of many islands. We flew around Malta, of course, an English base.

Before we landed in Tripoli, the plane flew a loop over the countryside, the town and the desert. Palm trees, huts, square houses built with a flat roof. I cannot yet say more. It is Africa, as you know it from pictures.

Tripoli — a town of 105,000 inhabitants, 30,000 Italians, Libyans, the latter poorly dressed. In the streets many 'soldiers', whites, blacks, Italians, sailors also, a few Germans in their new uniforms. This is particularly striking. Constant coming and going. In the streets, of course, no discipline. The chauffeur had to use his horn repeatedly to get through.

I went to see Rommel, who did not know that I already arrived and had been officially transferred to his staff. He was very pleased. In his great joy, he had informed me about everything, about which, of course, I cannot write. Sorry. You can be sure, my dear, that he will realise his objective. Already in these days, he has already achieved a great deal. Maybe you can read between the lines.

Rommel is an impressive and also an impressing personality. If only our troops would arrive here soon. The current difficulties of competence with the Italian troops were removed. They will, of course, never stop. Rommel has great plans.

So, now I have to go to the common meal, it is 19.30 hours. There will be a courier to Berlin. To you all, my beloved, many affectionate greetings, and for you much more from a foreign country. Your loving Jochen.

Tripoli, 22 February 1941

. . .

In eight days, we won't be here any more. The situation changes from day to day, i.e., if the weather is nice, and the regular shipments arrive at the port. Yesterday a transport ship on its return was sunk by an English submarine. We were already surprised on the plane to see that the convoy was accompanied by only three instead of four vessels. The fourth ship had already been sunk. It was said, however, that later the Italian torpedo boats accompanying the convoy had sunk the English submarine.

We hope that the protection of transport vessels will be efficient enough for the military units to cross the Mediterranean.

When you get this letter, it will probably have been in the newspaper that we are called the 'Afrika Korps'. Rommel is commander of the

Deutsches Afrika Korps (DAK).

In Africa, of course, you have to deal with great distances, and hence time. Today at lunch Rommel goes by plane to the front to introduce General Streich. It is about 800 km to the front. From farmer to farmer or from water source to water source the distances are impressive. This is called a populated area. The distances with their impact on calculating times are among the key elements of our strategic planning.

For me, there is still some idling. At the moment my office is organised: there's a table and chair, there is also enough paper. The entire staff will be composed in Berlin. I am glad I brought Pfistermeister [his aide] with me; he looks after my affairs.

The front side of the hotel faces the harbour. It offers a very nice view over the sea. No waves, some ships in the port. A hospital ship went down just before the harbour entrance on a mine. This time I should have taken a camera with me. But I will later ask Rommel for photos – he has already shot many pictures.

If Tripoli is a 'modern metropolis', I can't guess what kind of Africa we are going to see. In the desert you can't, of course, expect too much.

My hotel room opens to the east and is pleasantly cool. The heat is thus acceptable. Air raid warning. A single English plane, probably a reconnaissance aircraft, was shelled by the anti-aircraft units. Everything was over within five minutes.

They say that I should accompany Rommel today. Departure at 14.45 return tomorrow.

Tripoli, 24 February 1941

. . .

Air raid warning at this moment. It is 21.30 so there is no light. I am sitting in my room lit by candlelight. The English planes will be coming, suspecting vessels in port or having seen a convoy at sea assumed to be on its way here.

On Saturday afternoon, I accompanied Rommel and General Streich to Syrte, about 480 km, to visit the local positions. We returned at 19.15, in the dark.

The landscape is definitely very much bleaker than I ever imagined. On the coast about 100 km from here are new settlements built by Il Duce, palm plantations close by. When I was just peacefully writing this letter, I heard a plane. As I did not hear any shots, I assumed first that it was one of our aircraft and the air-raid warning that went off was wrong. False. A minute later, shooting everywhere.

On the following morning about 8.30 hours we flew to the front unit in the middle of the desert. There was a good atmosphere and a lot of momentum, even though the Italian catering is more than poor: dry mouldly bread, for dipping into edible oil, butter substitute, plus canned meat. That was our lunch. If the commander is in control, then he can help to get over such shortcomings with verve and authority.

When we arrived, a reconnaissance party, whose soldiers made an excellent impression, left the camp. As we heard later in Tripoli, it was quite successful. It destroyed English tanks and took prisoners. That's a great performance, to cover 200 km in the desert and find the enemy.

After the sumptuous lunch and a tour of the entire installation, we flew to three oases. We landed at one of them and were welcomed by Italian soldiers stationed there. They were visibly pleased that we had come. They probably didn't expect German officers – even the Commander – to visit. Then we flew to Sirte, were served rice soup and tea from the field hospital and spent the night over there. Next morning back in Tripoli.

So I travelled at least 1,500 km by air and several kilometres in a car in the desert. This first exploration was quite impressive and interesting.

Rommel seems to be content that I am here. Tomorrow morning I have no special programme. Around 14.00 hours Rommel will visit the south by plane. We shall be back in the evening.

The supplies coming from Italy are not really working as they should yet. The protection of the convoys by the Italian navy seems to improve, so, hopefully, all ships will arrive. The English, however, are trying their best to prevent it. Yesterday an Italian merchant ship carrying frozen meat was torpedoed, but it managed to enter the harbour.

. . .

That should really be everything today. But we have just been bombed. Bombs are still falling. A ship in the port was hit and is burning. Three places in town are burning, probably in the Arab quarter. I suppose that the English aircraft stopped over in Malta. I cannot imagine how so many bombs can be carried so far. I can hear even more explosions. The attack has already lasted 90 minutes.

Tripoli, 25 February 1941

. . .

Last night was another disturbed one. English aircraft appeared again at 3.30 hours and bombed us. From my window, about 600 m away, a commercial steamer was burning at sea still this morning, until it finally turned on its side and sank. I had expected at least one reconnaissance plane this morning, but so far none has shown up. But transport ships were able to enter the harbours and are now unloaded. Friedrich [code name for Rommel] has not taken off; the situation was probably not safe enough for the Italians. The weather is uniformly good so that probably wasn't the reason.

Beginning next week Rommel plans to go Berlin to report to the Führer and on his return to meet Il Duce. His programme is always full. The general situation is unchanged.

Rommel has just returned from an inspection of the Italian troops. He did not look satisfied with it, as far as I could tell.

How will the situation develop, and what will the English do? Will they fight in Greece or turn against us in North Africa? I am convinced that they will bombard us more often at night. Though their planes were shelled yesterday significantly, they were able to get away without important losses.

. . .

Tripoli, 26 February 1941

. . .

Today, we have been mentioned in the Army Report for the first time, 'at the Libyan front'.

Later Rommel and Colonel von dem Borne, the corps chief, and I drove to the port to observe the unloading of ships, which progressed quickly. The ships entered the port yesterday evening. The sight of a transport entering the port is really a solemn moment.

We are very happy about it – not only because the troops are here and available now, but because they crossed the Mediterranean safely and were not caught by the English submarines lying in wait. At the time outside the port entrance seven English submarines were waiting until they were driven off by the torpedo boats with depth-charges.

An Italian cruiser of the convoy was sunk by the English. Hence we are always very anxious to know whether the shipments arrive all right. Yesterday we expected aircraft over night, because they would have found targets inside the port. But they did not come, and it was calm. It surprised us, because they should really have known that the ships would enter here. Tonight the ships are unloaded and go back tomorrow.

Today again an Italian convoy has arrived. It will be unloaded tomorrow. Another battalion comes tomorrow. Hopefully, it will carry on like that. Rommel mentioned at breakfast that our service in the tropics would continue into the future – but my hopes were for something else!

. . .

Tripoli, 28 February 1941

. . .

My mission to explore and set up our next position in Sirte was quickly accomplished. I was happy therefore that I could return on Rommel's plane from the front. Rommel piloted the plane, actually quite well, even if his steering considerably shook us up several times.

Tomorrow, the Italians have arranged a big parade. Rommel, Borne and I are invited to it and to a following breakfast given by the commander of Tripoli, Excellence Guerra, at 13.00 hours. Unfortunately, I don't understand much Italian.

Rommel will probably start for Berlin next Monday and at the earliest be back after five days. Until then, we believe, that there will probably be no big changes in the general situation.

. . .

The battalion arriving yesterday has already moved to the front. The next transport is expected to come on Sunday. The English have not attacked the transports, and have left us in peace. Our aircraft can cause them considerable losses. Our anti-aircraft units downed an English Blenheim yesterday near Sirte .

For two weeks, the English have not moved forward. They would have got a nice response. Meanwhile, we are already so strong that they would suffer heavy losses. If only our tanks would come! Then we could advance.

Tripoli, 1 March 1941

. . .

Rommel is very tense. He has again postponed his planned trip to Berlin.

He puts pressure on everything. In eight days, new shipments will arrive.

This morning, I had breakfast with him. Afterwards we took the salute of the Italian artillery regiment with Gariboldi followed by a parade march. I will abstain from any judgement, but I do hope that their fighting quality is better.

A huge and enthusiastic crowd had gathered for the parade on both sides of the street. Excellence Gariboldi handed over to Rommel a brand new caravan with sofa, folding bed, table, two cabinets, toilet, shower, electric light and water pump. Our command car, arriving with staff from Berlin, will be so primitive and simple that nothing can be achieved with it. The Afrika Korps only gets what Berlin reserves for us, and we have to accept it.

After the parade we had breakfast given by the commander of Tripoli; it was a rich breakfast, as usual for the Italians, with innumerable courses. The Italians eat always well: as hors d'oeuvre ham, then soup, rice, eggs, meat on toast, a sweet egg dish, fruits, cheese, red wine, Italian sparkling wine, mocha, liqueur. The whole thing lasted for two hours. But you feel uncomfortable, if you can't have a discussion. Many Italians understand German quite well, but do not speak it, though they speak French.

. . .

Gradually one comes round to the idea, that even after peace one might stay here in Africa, temporarily. Who else would become the occupation force in the colonies? Our next location could be Dar es Salaam or Cairo or any other place. A stay of two to three years in Africa would be not too bad. In days that are constantly beautiful you can have more fun in life than during the long bad-weather periods we get in our country!

Tripoli, 2 March 1941

. . .

My thoughts returned to you. Fourteen days ago today, a Sunday, we were together for the last time in our own four walls. It will be a long time before this will be possible again. I console myself by thinking that my transfer here is very honourable and probably crucial for my career. One should not try to change by force the ways of fate. Wait and see.

I just heard that German troops have entered Bulgaria, cheered on by the population! The English know, of course. What will they undertake now? This invasion is also very important to our front. They will be careful to attack us here in Africa, but will be satisfied to keep up with the situation, as long as we do not attack them. Yesterday, one of our reconnaissance parties captured another English lieutenant and a sergeant.

One might expect a lot of us, but of course not everything can be quickly settled. The distances in the desert are large, and the few existing water points have been destroyed by the Italians during their retreat. And without water nothing will be working.

. . .

Tripoli, 4 March 1941

. . .

In the evening I stayed at the port as another convoy entered it. Tonight the next one should come. But it will take a while until we are in a position to intervene with the planned forces to advance up to Benghazi. The huge distance can only be overcome with great difficulty. We advanced to the new front position without any problems yesterday.

Rommel is in constant correspondence with Hitler's adjutant. But there are still many questions to be clarified that can only be discussed verbally.

Tomorrow, a film on the western front and our victory will be shown; the Italian officers and their wives are invited. I know the film. The war is something else, and not as harmless as it is depicted in it.

. . .

Tripoli, 5 March 1941

. . .

As we came back from our daily port visit, Rommel was already back from his trip back to the front. Enthusiastic. Now, our front units are positioned 750 km from here as the crow flies.

Tripoli, 6 March 1941

. . .

Still one point, my beloved, don't feel worried that we advance so slowly. The preparations, although they are done by Rommel, you may imagine, are enormous, and we cannot start before the difficult question of supplies is fully organised. We are not fighting in a developed region, where even if everything is destroyed, one still can find something useful, but we are in a desert of thousands of kilometres. But when we start, everything will be ready.

If we deploy our full forces, then it is likely that there will be no more problems in this theatre. Everything will proceed as planned. Furthermore, there are more divisions to come. But that might still take some time.

We have already achieved a lot: the Italian troops, which before our arrival planned to retire to Tripoli to defend the town, which never would have been successful, are now about 500 km away and our troops 750 km from us at the front. The advance of the English troops was stopped! A great success. But we have still to become much stronger and secure the supplies. You, at home, you will still have to wait for a while. But in autumn, we shall certainly be in Cairo!

Before dinner, I walked with Rommel for a half an hour. Again, he indicated clearly how happy he is about the mission. He is right to think so.

. . .

Tripoli, 7 March 1941

. . .

The morning passed quickly. After breakfast I drove down to the port with General Streich. Supplies were unloaded again, a routine by now. Rommel is currently with His Excellence Gariboldi, who has been visiting the Italian units in the last two days. An Italian division was put under Rommel's command. One step forward. We continue to progress, step by step.

The next transport will soon bring us the panzers, which will lift the fighting morale of the Italians: it has gone down because of the defeats the Italians are suffering now. Recently, four panzers were unloaded. That was sensational, half the population came to watch. They hadn't seen anything like it here before. But no matter what, unless the supply issues are completely resolved and fixed, fighting cannot begin. Shipments should come much more frequently. But the transport yesterday arrived without being bothered by the English.

Yesterday morning, two British planes flew over the town. But last night was calm, although transport ships loaded with troops and supplies were in port. Only donkeys screamed, dogs barked and cats miaowed – as they do, by the way, every night.

Departure for the desert begins in a day or two, for the staff as well, including my office, but in phases.

. . .

Tripoli, 8 March 1941

. . .

Yesterday the welcome of German troops and the review took place without Rommel. Excellence Gariboldi welcomed the units, and took the salute. It worked perfectly. The Italian police and the music corps begin to know our way of organising the review of troops. The next review in Tripoli will not be organised by me, as I shall leave next Monday at 5.00 hours for Sirte, about 480 km away from here, the road is good.

Today and tomorrow I will still enjoy my hotel room and the magnificent tiled bathroom. The day after tomorrow this kind of luxury will be over with, along with the agreeable aspects of civilised life for a while. Maybe the English have not completely destroyed Benghazi. We will probably not stay for very long in Sirte.

Tonight the English bombed us four times, each time for perhaps twenty minutes. Although the port was filled with transport ships and other vessels, they did not cause any damage. Half-moon and parachute flares covered the area in daylight. The anti-aircraft units fired incessantly.

. . .

Still in Tripoli, 9 March 1941

. . .

Yesterday evening, it was already quite muggy, during the day we had 33° in the shade, inside the hotel 40°. For us the mission is beginning: in the hotel we always had fresh rooms to work in, but this will finish now. Instead we must put on our tropical helmets. Today for the first time I put on my tropical uniform. Rommel said that I looked very decent, and he was angry that he had not yet got *his* tropical uniform.

Rommel seems to plan to go to Berlin only after the arrival of the panzers, probably in about eight to ten days. Until 21.30 hours the corps chief and I sat together with him. It was nice and enjoyable. He was again filled with a thousand new ideas. I have never met anyone until now as agile in thinking and acting as him. He is fully engaged by the fulfilment of his mandate, he sets an example rarely encountered.

He lives for this mission. Ideas originate in his head, which, if implemented, would contribute to reaching the goal. It is interesting to witness. I, personally, am not so interested in constantly listening to the analytical evaluation of current events.

The corps chief just told me that the departure of the staff is postponed for one day. The panzers will arrive later. Rommel really wanted to welcome them by a parade in Tripoli. We wait for them to arrive impatiently: their presence will not only affect the attitude of the Italians but will have a special effect of encouraging them and at the same time offering relief. But the convoy had to return twice to Naples owing to bad weather. Furthermore, in an incident we don't have details of some tanks burned when being loaded. We are worried.

I was hardly in bed last night when the first attack came. It rained bombs. After a pause, the second attack, and at 2.00 hours, the third and last. The anti-aircraft units shot fervently, splinters dropped down on the street. As I learned this morning, the shooting lasted until 3.30 a.m. I am amazed that I slept solidly, as most anti-aircraft guns are positioned around the port, therefore close to my hotel.

. . .

Today, three weeks have passed since we were together. How many more lots of three weeks have still to elapse! I suppose in July, when it will be 50° in the shade, a pause will occur, in which one might take leave. But wait, for the question of leave depends on the overall situation, and it is wrong to think about it.

. . .

Still in Tripoli, 10 March 1941

. . .

After lunch, to which Rommel had invited the Italian liaison officer, Excellence Calvi, the king's son-in-law, twenty-six officers and civil servants suddenly arrived, as well as thirty-one officers of the armed force. The first group was transferred to the staff and had to be accommodated. Now, the staff consists of forty officers and civil servants who have not yet found the routine of coordinated working. I regretted not having had time to join Rommel to go to the port. The first company of a panzer regiment had arrived. Likewise, I missed the presentation of the panzers and the Italian parade, where I was supposed to accompany Rommel.

Getting used to the work and cooperating together happens much quicker than at home. We have to rely on each other in this country

The date of my departure was again postponed for twenty-four hours because the parade of panzers will only take place the day after tomorrow, on Wednesday. Excellence Gariboldi will not be here tomorrow. Moreover, he wanted the participation of Italian troops.

. . .

Still in Tripoli, 11 March 1941

. . .

Rommel is considering a complete block on leave. He thinks that instead one could set up a holiday rest home somewhere on the coast. Wives could come there. Such a plan will provoke protests. Recreation after a long deployment in another country is only possible at home. A holiday rest home would be nothing better than a brothel. Staying in this country would also not completely cut off military life. Also, one has to consider the majority of reservists who need to take care of their farms and enterprises during their leave.

Today Rommel has flown to the front again and will come back tomorrow. Major Appel, from the war college at Wiener Neustadt, who has wanted for a long time to be transferred to Rommel and who arrived yesterday, will accompany him.

Rommel was in a bad mood today. He did not sleep well. He goes to bed quite early, but gets up early. At night he needs calm, but he does not find it because of the permanent air raids. Yesterday, the English bombed twice, once tonight, only 500 m away as the crow flies. They destroyed a hangar. The anti-aircraft units shot more than ever before. Afterwards it is often difficult to fall asleep again.

. . .

Sirte, 13 March 1941

. . .

During my last night in the hotel in Tripoli another alarm, for the first time even before the anti-aircraft units started shooting. But no aircraft came. So I continued sleeping until Pfistermeister woke me up at 4.00 hours. Around 5.15 we left by vehicle for Sirte bypassing Hemi, Missureta and Bueret.

What I had already seen from the plane looked quite different when passing the landscape in the car. On the way, Aldinger [Rommel's aide] tried to take a photo of an Arab woman. Although he approached her as if he was stalking a deer, it was impossible. The woman ran away, left her oxen at the well and was not seen again. Arabs came running, demanding cigarettes. They did not succeed in getting the woman back either. After we had left these inhabited sites, there was more bleak desert, sand and sand, terribly boring.

In Sirte, the Italian officers invited us to their mess for lunch. Compared to the quality offered in Tripoli, there was only one difference: Instead of oranges for dessert, orange jam was offered. The Italian officers live very well, while the ordinary ranks have to be content with lesser fare, with bread and canned meat and red wine.

Yesterday afternoon we were waiting for Rommel and Borne, supposed to arrive by plane, but a sandstorm threatened. The sun clouded over and the sandstorm was fierce. Dry sand penetrated mouth, nose, eyes – just everywhere. One could partly see two metres ahead. I went to the airfield. The head of the air traffic control office told me that only one machine was in the air. He refused it permission to land.

Later I heard that a Ju [Junckers, German aircraft] wanted to land. It could only be Rommel. After illuminating navigational lights, which the pilot did not see as he later told us, the plane landed. The passengers were a sergeant and two non-commissioned officers, whose presence in the air no one knew about. A flight without permission – there would be consequences for these three. But where was Rommel's plane? He arrived later, at midnight, by car.

An Italian major, who has been living in Libya for twenty-five years, and other officers confirmed that they had never before known such a *ghibli* [sandstorm]. We, members of the staff, have been quite well off until now, because are living in buildings, but the soldiers at the front are in tents . . . Everywhere in our office was covered in sand, centimetres deep; it was even on our desks despite closed windows, shutters and doors. We experienced the worst kind of *ghibli* at the outset here, and it would be not be a surprise in future. It is annoying that there is no – or only very little – water for cleaning.

. . .

Sirte, 16 March 1941

. . .

On mission in Tripoli: at a late hour, Caminesci appeared at the hotel, Cavalry Regiment Stolp, dirty like a desert-front soldier. He had been at the front. Although we only knew each other a bit, it was a warm reunion. The desert brings people together.

Overnight another two serious bomb attacks . . . With each shot the windows panes rattled. Then again bombs. Splinters fell on the pavement.

Back in Sirte: it was not a quiet Sunday. Hopefully, the English will not come. During last night they bombed the airfield. At the front where our panzers are positioned English air raids have killed and wounded the first soldiers. Unfortunately, no English aircraft had been shot down. It could be that the English will attack us. Their preparations seem to have become more intensified. But it will be in vain. Rommel will probably leave for Rome and Berlin in a few days, after the arrival of the panzers at the front. Tomorrow morning he will first drive to two Italian divisions under the command of the Afrika Korps. There is still much to do.

. . .

Sirte, 17 March 1941

. . .

My office is functional again so I can begin writing today's letter. Later I have to meet Rommel to get his signature – he left early this morning. Earlier I went on 260 km ahead with the corps chief to have a look at the spot selected to be the headquarters. It is in the countryside. Our tents, on the other hand, we want to install in the dunes close to the beach in a bay. The beach is wonderful. The office will be installed in a small house, 400 metres off the road.

Tripoli was exposed again to a three-hour air raid yesterday night. We had a peaceful night. The English certainly won't find us in our hidey-hole on the beach.

Yet we have sometimes the feeling that the English would like to attack us here. I can't believe that the British would dare to.

Yesterday, an aircraft, a Junckers which I used the day before yesterday was attacked by a Blenheim, but without success. Two officers of our flight squadron recently flew into a *ghibli* and did not return. It is supposed that the aircraft downed in the sea.

Sirte, 18 March 1941

. . .

I really couldn't imagine that Rommel would free himself to make time to go to Berlin to report personally on the situation. But he believes it is the right moment. According to a message, the situation has already changed again. I do not believe that operations will wait much longer. Rommel does not have the patience to wait until everything has arrived. He will attack at a favourable opportunity. And it seems that the moment approaches.

Today, at 10.00 hours our anti-aircraft unit has downed a Blenheim. First information spoke of two, but one slipped away. But it was certainly one of those who had attacked the units at the front yesterday, so that we had dead and wounded. With the return of Rommel from Berlin the last panzers of the armoured regiment will be at the front.

Today at lunch, I learned something. We had pea soup, but the peas were hardly edible. They were hard despite long cooking. Why? Because our water is too salty. The water issue, the most important question in the desert, will often create us great difficulties.

. . .

Sirte, 19 March 1941

. . .

The night was quite troubled again. I don't know how often the English have bombed us; I assume they came at least five times, and even relatively low. The anti-aircraft units, under Italians command, shot, but not too often, they will probably not have brought one plane down. They covered the airfield with fire bombs.

. . .

Sirte, 20 March 1941

. . .

Should the English continue to retreat, Rommel will go forward with the troops available to him – I had often seen him do this in France. We have to get hold of the English so that we can wipe them out. But what do the English intend by withdrawing? And where are they going? And we have to ask, which target we will pursue. Instructions will be probably given to Rommel in Berlin now.

. . .

I continue to hope that I will see Cairo. Otherwise my trip here won't have been worth it.

Today, I went up to the front, some 100 km out, to find out whether Casa Ristoro could be our next headquarters. But what are 100 km! We are well-equipped with aircraft to find airfields anywhere: these are extended by the Italians with amazing speed. The construction of airfields in the desert is not too difficult. The Italians are excellent road builders.

Sirte, 22 March 1941

. . .

With comments about others, coming to one's ears, one should be careful. However, they are always interesting. The corps chief is considered to be too hesitant. That is not correct, in my opinion. He is clever and considered and is an excellent counterweight to Rommel.

The transport of units and supplies to the front is not easy to organise. Eight days ago, for example, a special mission began, on which 1,400 km were to be covered. These are the distances we constantly have to cope with. It's time consuming, everything takes longer. If we had begun preparing four or eight weeks ago, operations would already have started.

The time lost in advancing and on the supplies must then be caught up again. The eight-week campaign Rommel had been thinking about some time ago is obviously not discussed any more. It is simply unthinkable. Nevertheless, I am convinced that finally everything will be much faster than we are now assuming.

What makes everything more difficult is, of course, the fact that there is nothing available in this area which could be used for the advance. Everything has to be carried over hundreds of kilometres. In France, for example, we could always find food or petrol, even vehicles, which could be used instead of own vehicles which had broken down.

I have laid out the magazines you sent in the mess. They are very popular, everybody has been reading them. This week we might get newspapers.

. . .

Sirte, 23 March 1941

. . .

The planned transfer of our staff tomorrow 160 km closer to the front was postponed.

Were you not also surprised that Rommel got decorated with the Oak Leaves? *We* were quite surprised when the news came yesterday, and I immediately congratulated him by telex in Wiener Neustadt. We did not expect the message and are happy about it. But we are not clear why he has received it at this moment.

Undoubtedly, Rommel by his arrival finally stopped the retreat of the Italian army and hindered the English coming to Tripoli. But you might assume that an award comes only after a success and we would have advanced 1,000 km more. I am curious to see what Rommel brings along from Berlin. I am convinced that he will start soon. He has certainly accelerated the arrival of the next division. The award means certainly that the Führer agrees with his actions.

I will not make you feel discouraged over this period, but will console you because we shall certainly spend my birthday in October together! Rommel expects that the war will end before winter. I am also convinced of that. In this sense, I hope that you will pass an agreeable Sunday without lacking anything.

. . .

Sirte, 24 March 1941

. . .

The commando has worked assiduously. The house, my future office, is fairly clean. The tents in the dunes are installed, a large barracks has been built and a second will follow today. In the dunes there is a plethora of sand fleas, very small animals that you only can feel when, full of blood and the size of small peas, they abandon your body leaving fierce itching. The pioneers suffered most: the ones with bites swim in the sea, which is painful because of the strong salinity of the water. I looked, therefore, for another spot. But there were scorpions. They only bite when they are harassed, pressed or walked on. Their bites can be deadly. This area is full of surprises.

In Sirte, I slept well until the aircraft came between 3.45 and 4.45 a.m. and bombed us heavily. As they dropped fire bombs near my room it became bright as day despite closed shutters, so I got up. We stood close to the door, and we ducked our heads when two bombs fell in the immediate vicinity, about 100 feet from us, on a number of eucalyptus trees covering a parking area. An Italian unit was camping there.

Fifteen soldiers were killed. The other bombs have probably not damaged anything. Our anti-aircraft unit was obviously inadequate. It could only shoot up to 2,200 metres, as I yesterday found out. They are installed on the hill, perhaps only 150 feet from here. It is a fact that the anti-aircraft guns attract the [enemy] aircraft. The pilot thinks that where there is an anti-aircraft unit, there is something to protect. I think that we will soon leave this unfriendly region for the realm of the sand fleas.

Rommel has already come back at lunchtime today. He must have moved everything on. I didn't expect him until tonight. This morning he meets Gariboldi in Tripoli. I am curious what he will do during the next few days. With his return, life comes back to the staff.

Yesterday, a unit under the leadership of Major Appel on the way to Marada had contact with the enemy. The English destroyed two vehicles. Rommel will not be very happy about this. Rommel esteems Appel and believes that he can be trusted with any mission. Appel has always wanted to join a division. I have tried to be fair, because I did not believe that a man, who has been a commanding officer at the Military Academy in Wiener Neustadt, is necessarily suitable for every activity in a war. Rommel himself had requested his coming in Berlin. Appel was not very much at ease when he received this special order, because he had never before commanded such a unit. I feel very sorry for him that he had bad luck. I hope that he has not lost too many soldiers.

. . .

25 March 1941

. . .

In a hurry. In ten minutes captain Graf Baudissin will fly to Tripoli. So you will have at least a brief message from our new location in the dunes. El Agheila was occupied yesterday. The rapidly commanded relocation of the staff worked well. I slept for the first time in a tent in the dunes. Wonderful, without harassment by aircrafts, fleas or other vermin. The place is really superb.

Rommel is happy and has left already for El Agheila. The Führer was very happy, Mussolini much surprised. This morning at 7.00 hours, I swam in the Mediterranean. Morale is good everywhere.

. . .

26 March 1941

Dearest,

One should not believe that one has enough time here in the desert, the days are passing rapidly, they seem to be shorter, and because of lack of light at night one goes to bed early. I wanted to write you first about the events since 24 March. After lunch around 14.00 suddenly the command came from Rommel that the corps headquarters had to move, and march off in two hours.

Rommel himself was very happy when he returned from Berlin with his oak leaves. Last Thursday, he had interviews at the headquarters in Berlin, on Friday with the Führer, then a short visit to his family in Wiener Neustadt, on Saturday back to Rome, Sunday morning with Mussolini, in the afternoon in Tripoli, on Monday consultations in Tripoli, at noon in Sirte and in the evening at the new corps headquarters in the dunes.

The Führer was unreservedly satisfied with the achievements so far and the plans submitted to him. Rommel was told not to undertake any major operations.

All ministers assisted at a breakfast given by the Führer for Rommel. He was held in respect and the centre of attention. The atmosphere was especially agreeable.

Rommel had received the oak leaves for his deployment in France, not yet for Africa. The Grand Cross and rank of field marshal will probably come later! For me personally, this is of course very honourable!

The discussion with Mussolini was pleasant. Amazingly, he seemed in no way to be informed about developments on our side, neither about the shipments so far, our occupation of Marada, or further on, all important items for the campaign in North Africa. Il Duce must have been furious, as we already felt the impact. Marshal Graziani was firmly replaced by General Gariboldi as Governor General and army leader. Rommel will be very pleased with it.

The relocation passed without any problems. I gave orders according to my functions, packed my belongings and left in the direction of the front. Everything down to the smallest item was prepared by my vanguard. First came Rommel and Borne, delighted that everything been prepared in such detail.

Taking El Agheila happened without any problem. However, a panzer drove on a mine. The crew is dead, a panzer reconnaissance vehicle destroyed. Unfortunately the English escaped. El Agheila is a sad place, perhaps six simple Arab huts, two wells, a castle, some kind of a fortress of a very primitive construction, situated on a hill, an airfield without installations. That is all. Otherwise, we still find in the area remnants of the Italian retreat.

A propaganda film team filmed in El Agheila a lot as Rommel visited it yesterday morning. It is possible that something will turn up in the weekly newsreel.

. . .

27 March 1941

. . .

Last night it was insupportable in my tent. Since yesterday afternoon a *ghibli* raged in this region, which would stop you enjoying life. You are dirty as a pig, cannot use your eyes, your teeth gnash, you move only in dirt, because the rooms are full of dust and sand and your food is filled up with sand. When at 23.00 hours I crawled into my tent, a dusty cloud covered me. The fatigue quickly disappeared. But what can you do? So we slept in that dirt. And besides, the heat usually accompanying the *ghibli is* disagreeable.

. . .

Yesterday evening Rommel considered moving further forward with the staff. He changed his mind overnight. He preferred to stay here a bit longer. I have not yet spoken to him. He seems to think that life in the dunes should not go on too long. That night was really not pleasant. I will ask him whether he too swallowed sand in his beautiful caravan. Yesterday morning, he swam as early as at 6.00 a.m. and again in the afternoon.

28 March 1941

Dearest,

Yesterday evening, the corps chief, and also Baudissin, returned from Tripoli, but they did not bring any mail. Tomorrow Rommel will fly to Tripoli, returning in the evening. I think that he will fetch mail. Here in the desert especially one would like to receive even more letters than usual. Our life here is very simple and primitive. Food is moderate. Yesterday brown beans with water, many pieces of meat coming from an old oxen swimming in it.

I go here and there, hoping that the staff will function better from day to day. With respect to the high demands, I would prefer to have younger people around me, and not the tired reservists. They are good for playing *Skat* [German card game] at night. But I regret very much that I have not learned bridge. The corps chief would like to play it, but one person is always lacking. Yes, why have we not learned it? But in the time in our garrison town Stolp there was always so much going on that we didn't miss bridge. Otherwise, we would probably have had no more evenings at home.

It actually looks as if we will still remain here for a further four weeks. Later, when the real operations are going on, we shall follow the front. Then we won't have any more peacetime-style facilities around us. Everyone wants to have it like it is at home in peacetime.

. . .

29 March 1941

. . .

I know that you would like to send me something, you and the two boys. But you should not save up for me from your own reserves what you like to eat and what would be more useful for you. I organise myself quite well. Dear, I do tell you everything that preoccupies me, and I would write to you further, if I missed something. Our whole life and bustle are here quite simple and primitive, including meals. If one imagines that we live in the desert, 750 km away from a town, then we are well off.

30 March 1941

. . .

Today, once again Sunday. The day started quietly with beautiful weather. But now at 9.00 p.m. it is already over 25° – at noon it will be about 40° – it will be of no importance. We need heat after these stormy days, but not dust and dirt. Gradually, everybody becomes quiet and peaceful. Everybody is dependent on the other. It is of no use to make life harder mutually.

The equipment of the Italians with tents, field chairs and a kitchen is so incomparably more luxurious than ours. In their tents one can move, they are comfortable, with folding wash-stands and much more. The Italians have, of course, long experience in the desert. They know what one needs. In contrast, our place is rather primitive. Every Italian officer has cases, boxes of canned food, butter in cans, etc. Even our mess does not have these things.

Rommel did not return yesterday evening, we expect him now at 11.00. He has the consent of Gariboldi, and will probably soon get cracking. Only then will we have to think again of advancing the staff.

You wrote that you don't know the course of our front line. I am not allowed to tell you. But you have read in the Army Report that we have taken El Agheila, and that since then nothing else has happened. We have occupied Marada because it is situated at the southern tip of the so-called Salt Lake. We wish to prevent the English attacking us from below or from the side. Adjedabia is still at least 200 miles further on. According to the maps, which can be bought in Germany, you will not get a correct impression of the distances. The Army Report will have informed you that Adjedabia is still heavily bombarded.

The beginning of large operations has not yet come. I hope that it will be not too hot in four weeks. According to his nature Rommel is a hunter. He does it like a game, sleeping during daytime, moving at night. That certainly sounds very nice. But you know that there are circumstances and difficulties which have to be overcome.

Aldinger, appointed lieutenant, told me that he and Rommel were flying in thickest fog yesterday. They had the impression they came within a hair's breadth of death. It was gusty, so they had to fly very low. They survived by succeeding in passing the crest of the dunes and mountains.

We have not yet received German newspapers. But we can receive short wave. Since yesterday we are getting the Army Reports.

. . .

Adjedabia, 1 April 1941

Dearest,

It is the first of April. This year, you are safe from my jokes! Next year we shall be together again. Where? But the war can't last that long.

Sunday evening at 22.00 Rommel informed me that I should accompany him next day. I was, of course, delighted. The first major combat was planned. Departure at 6.00 with the corps chief to the division staff in El Agheila.

The operation turned out well after settling a few problems. Rommel

73

drove to the panzers at the front line, which could not advance on Marsa Brega; they were stopped by field fortifications, an anti-tank ditch installed by the English. Marsa Brega was occupied just before dusk. In the meantime, a nearby anti-aircraft battery had got into position, and was shelled by the English artillery. Some grenades landed close to us: one dead, several light and seriously wounded. Even the roof of my car was damaged by grenade fragments. I was not inside. Thus, we had to look several times for shelter.

I have admired Rommel's calm, and above all, that he did not even intervene. Taking Marsa Brega should have happened earlier. Later he told me that he as supreme commander could not have done it. But I am convinced that such a hesitant approach of the 7th Armoured Division in France would not have happened. The English, of course, have exploited this laxity and were shelling us considerably. Rommel wanted above all to prevent losses. It is, of course, possible that by another strategy more losses would have occurred. It is important, however, that we have taken this advanced position.

At the time of the action Rommel had the right feeling. The English were on the way to take back again either Marada or even Agheila.

. . .

Adjedabia, 3 April 1941

. . .

On Monday, Marsa Brega was occupied. During the night of Tuesday we moved forward, yesterday up to 30 km east of Adjedabia. The English continued to run away. We captured some 200 prisoners, including some officers. I do not believe that we advance already to Benghazi. Meanwhile, Tripoli is about 900 km away.

We have a terrible heat, with little wind, because we are no longer close to the sea. The troops are thirsty. As long as there are provisions in the mess, it may still go. But supply is missing. Still, we are all right.

Great rush yesterday when shifting the battle stand three times. In addition, dense traffic on the single road. Adjedabia as El Agheila are rather destroyed by artillery and Stukas [dive bombers]. During the day we are in town, at night we move in the desert. We learn by experience.

Yesterday night we were heavily bombed by the English, even though we were outside the town. Just like this morning, at low altitude.

Nevertheless, the anti-aircraft unit shot down none of the five aircraft! This is the latest news, in short as I am in a hurry.

Rommel is very nice to everybody. He seems to be very happy. We too, because, contrary to previous assumptions and intentions, everything passed more quickly and so far only with relatively few losses.

. . .

Adjedabia, 4 April 1941

. . .

In a hurry. Maybe you have heard on the radio the special message that Benghazi has been taken by us tonight. The headquarters will advance further today by passing south of Benghazi. I am very much concerned whether we have enough vehicles. The night before yesterday two cars were so badly damaged that they are unusable. Last night another car failed. The drivers escaped without being seriously hurt. Half an hour ago the command car of Lieutenant Colonel Ehlert went over a mine. And where will I get new ones? I shan't get them from the divisions, as they need every car.

The equipment of the corps staff is bad. The gentlemen in Berlin, having no notion of Africa and its local conditions, make financial savings in the wrong places. It will have consequences. I sent back my two trucks to collect equipment left behind. Twenty-four hours have passed and they have not yet come back, even though they only had to go a distance of 450 km. Worries, nothing but worries.

The English continue to pull back. Some less important engagements. Supply of water and fuel is difficult. I hope we can keep up the current pace. If we can we will be soon at the Egyptian border. But there are still 900 km to go.

Yesterday evening Excellence Gariboldi came to see Rommel. He had a very long, serious talk with him, but finally agreed with his plans. We demand a lot from our soldiers. But Rommels' intention is right, to go forward now and remain close at the enemy. Today, it was again very hot, 40° to 45°, practically no wind, during the night, on the other hand, very cold.

. . .

Adjedabia, 5 April 1941

. . .

We are still in Adjedabia. Actually, we should have left yesterday afternoon. This morning it was said that the decision will be taken after Rommel's return from the front.

Everything is excellent. We cannot go forward very quickly as the English run away. We also cannot advance frontally, but must try again and again, by sending units or divisions in the desert to attack the English in their flank to cut them off the road. This slows down our advance. Moreover, we must do everything possible to ensure that the English disappear from the desert. This can't be guaranteed if we follow them only on the only existing road.

The advance is much faster than it could have been foreseen. The supply of water and fuel confronts us with serious difficulties because the main operation should only begin not earlier than end of April.

This day seems to become decisive. It seems possible to push through the desert coming from the south to the sea close to Tobruk–Derna. Then we could cut off the withdrawal of one part of the English troops.

This morning, shortly after 4.00 a.m., Rommel sent his aide to wake me up to move off with one part of the command 500 km away. Well, I had the impression that the decision was premature, as the corps staff as such moves only earliest in the afternoon, perhaps only tomorrow. We could perhaps advance even beyond Benghazi.

. . .

Comrades described the great joy of the inhabitants of Benghazi when we were marching in. The ordinary people expressed their joy by getting drunk. The soldiers were covered with flowers, beer was offered, etc.

Apparently only the power station and waterworks are destroyed. Otherwise, the town made a good impression. I have sent two cars to fetch beer and mineral water. Both products have become rare in the mess.

. . .

Adjedabia, 5 April 1941

. . .

Tomorrow in eight days it is Easter already. Probably not one of us would have thought of it. I would like to send you, my love, and to the boys my heartfelt wishes for very happy holidays.

I assume that in eight days, we will be much further on, perhaps at a place where we can also go swimming. Here, we are still lucky because there are some wells. But the water must be boiled. But it is water. In the desert, standards are very low. One becomes modest when living in dirty surroundings.

Otherwise, only a few things happened this morning.

Gariboldi appeared suddenly at noon. The consultation was short and ended on 'by mutual agreement and the spirit and confidence of the common victory', as newspapers say, formulating it beautifully. Afterwards Rommel and the corps chief flew to the front immediately. Do we come now to the sea and do we capture a good number of English soldiers?

Yesterday evening for the first time we received complete radio news: long reports about the occupation of Benghazi. According to the contents of these reports one could conclude that in these days we had acquired particularly large spoils of war. The five fingers of a hand are sufficient enough to enumerate them. The English had planned the retreat and – as it seems – even withdrawn in full order.

Our difficulties are the water supply and the supply of fuel. This is particularly true for the units crossing the desert on camel tracks. It is not fast, especially not with the Italians. If we had here instead of just one German division four more, the situation would probably be different.

This afternoon I captured a truck from the Royal Air Force. It will be very useful for us! Another three Volkswagens should be coming from Tripoli. They will solve my transportation problems. But every morning I hear the same thing, that during the night another car broke down.

Graf Baudissin is missing. He had to make an emergency landing in the desert. He probably will be found with the help of radio contact.

. . .

Adjedabia, 12 April 1941

Dearest,

I could not write you since Sunday because I have been in the desert until Wednesday night on a special mission. Afterwards I had to go with Rommel immediately to the front. Back late at night. Overnight planes and ships fired at us that I could not think of writing one letter. I have not yet been able to read your letters, received yesterday evening. Do not be sad, my heart, I am well.

We advance with great speed. The English are withdrawing, although they fight very bravely. I hope that today you will be pleased with the special message that we have taken Tobruk. I hope that you are all well and that you passed nice Easter.

. . .

Adjedabia, 12 April 1941

. . .

I did not go with the general as I preferred to bring some order into my unit. It was necessary. And last but not least, I wanted to read your letters calmly and give you a report for which you have certainly waited already.

. . .

But believe me that I thought every day how to send you a letter. It was not possible.

. . .

Sending it by plane was not possible, as there were no planes.

This morning at 6.30 hours I had just left Rommel's vehicle when a plane turning like a gyroscope at about 100 m altitude fell to the ground like a stone 50 m in front of me. One man dead, the other badly injured. That was the morning surprise.

In short, last night was as violent as I have ever experienced before. Around 24.00, I lay down in my tent; I had hardly read two letters, when the first air raid came, then shots from English ships in between, followed by aircraft attacking us from low altitude with machine guns. It was a terrible noise. It is possible that the English knew where we were.

How long all this noise actually took, I do not know, I fell asleep, I was just tired, woken only up now and again when a bomb exploded nearby. Moreover, I felt safe as I was in a hollow, quite distant, which Pfistermeister had selected.

. . .

In any case, an incredible night.

Yesterday we proceeded as planned, the attack on the whole front line should have started at 16.00, but the panzers were not advancing. The English artillery shot heavily on us, Rommel, Corps Chief von dem Borne and I were quite surprised about the resistance. Our strategy was not good in general, because I believe that the tanks were not aggressive enough. If they had attacked aggressively, Tobruk would have fallen. I am convinced of it. I am surprised that Rommel stayed calm. I know him well and would have expected otherwise. Many vehicles and soldiers remained entrenched, simply accepting the strong artillery fire.

. . .

As today we have occupied Bardia, I am somewhat consoled. This is a present for Easter for you at home! Now, it will not take much longer before we will, after having freed Cyrenaica of the enemy, move on to the Egyptian border, and then from Alexandria to Cairo. The division needs rest and supplies, but it would be wrong to give up pursuing the English. You will ask for losses: frankly, I do not know . . . But I have the impression that they are moderate. But the many English bombs and low-altitude attacks caused relatively many losses.

Major General von Prittwitz und Gaffron, commander of the 15th Armoured Division, which has not yet all arrived, only parts, has been killed. He advanced too far, a shell of the English artillery hit him in his car and he was killed instantly. Yesterday evening I had to write a sad letter to his wife. The radio message ahead will probably arrive just for Easter. Very sad. Officer losses are otherwise tolerable.

Our destroyed vehicles are replaced by excellent English cars, so that some German unities will not be recognised as German, and one might think that there are English here. Besides, our men can barely be identified, covered by dirt and dust. Well, my dear, I need to go back to the passed days in this letter, so that you will know what I have been doing from Sunday to Thursday.

. . .

On Sunday morning, the staff was ready to advance in the direction of the front; Rommel and Borne have not come back for already nearly forty-eight hours and Ehlert ordered me to move with the corps headquarters by passing Solluch-Smus-Fengeder to Gadd el Amar, about 500 km with the intention of relocating the corps headquarters there, but also to strengthen the right flank (with the corps staff, bus, command vehicle and a Fla. MG Kp. [flak-gun company] with 12.2-cm guns).

After quick preparations for fuel and water enough for 500 km, I left at 11:00. We were a strange group. No sooner I had left the coastal road to Benghazi for the desert, I was in a sandstorm, which was worse than the one in Adjedabia. I met Italian units of the Division Ariete, which should be, according to Ehlert, already in Gadd el Amar. During a *ghibli* Italians generally stop. Contrary to the view of the Italian liaison command that went with me, I continued and arrived in Smus around 19:30. Well, I was very surprised myself that I found this spot faster than others. I stayed there overnight.

Next morning I crossed the desert following the compass and the sun, withstood three air raids, but I had five soldiers wounded. From that moment, I was almost constantly accompanied by English aircraft. The third day again a savage sandstorm that reduced visibility to 2 metres.

We were crossing an area of stones in a mountainous region awfully difficult to pass, nothing but stones when just for a moment it became bright, I saw a sign, a sign in the desert, I drove to it and read: Gadd El Ahmar. I was told to go there, and I had found something that no one had found before me or behind me. I installed some artillery on top of the hill and felt relatively safe. As I know now, I should have been worried, because that area was full of English tanks. I also sent out a reconnaissance party – one came back with a captain and six Canadians as prisoners . . .

I liked this tour. I felt master of that desert area. The soldiers were loyal and enthusiastic despite water shortages. The water reserves taken along were not sufficient by far, fuel was only just enough. Two days after I had radio contact with Ehlert; he was happy and proud that I had arrived while the Italians arrived only four days later. Although I had first lost a lot of vehicles on the first couple of days, but since yesterday, they are all back again, repaired, having come with other units.

. . .

I could, of course, give a much longer report of this trip; it was a real desert ride with completely inadequate, overloaded vehicles in an extremely difficult area. But I had fulfilled my mission. I had much luck, but I am proud of my success. And Ehlert is proud especially, because he was right, as Rommel had criticised him for sending the corps headquarters into the desert. But it was for me an interesting mission which I enjoyed very much. Fuel and water, I finally got by air and I had two wonderful days after my arrival. I would like to do something like it again. My excursion has become widely known. Corps staff far ahead the fighting force. Rommel was happy that I was back.

. . .

Near Tobruk, 14 April 1941

. . .

Yesterday, Easter, preparations to attack the fortress of Tobruk, defended by the English with tenacity. Individual attack attempts have been in vain. Since 6.oo our units have been attacking in close formation. They seem to be advancing. The English artillery, which has harassed us for days, isn't firing any more.

Easter did not exist for us. It is cold, perhaps only 12°, so we are running around in thick coats. Strong, dusty winds. We are doing well. Colonel Knabe has occupied Sollum yesterday. I think that Tobruk will fall afterwards. I hope that it will be soon warmer for our entry into Egypt.

I think of you a lot. How are you?

Outside Tobruk, 15 April 1941

. . .

Yesterday I could not write you a long letter. I did not have the calm I needed for it. Constant artillery fire and bombs until evening. It was not good at all. My thoughts were with you. Tobruk has not yet been taken. Yesterday's attack of the heavily reinforced town could not bring success. The English immediately closed the breach. What was in there remained inside. Our soldiers probably went into captivity. Today the English artillery did not shoot.

. . .

Overnight it was relatively calm. But just now again five bombers were back on us and have bombed. Today it is not so cloudy, so perhaps the anti-aircraft unit will have more success. We need a second German division. We are very annoyed by Italian army reports. The brave Italian soldiers run just away and cannot be held back once shots are fired. We simply can't afford to leave the strategically important Tobruk behind us while we are advancing. Since yesterday afternoon we have been positioned in a hollow, buried in.

Outside Tobruk, 15 April 1941

. . .

The supply of our troops is not in step with our advance. We live almost exclusively on English rationing. It is very good. Even the food of our field kitchen is improved by English spoils.

My love, you believe that the beginning of the operation was ordered by Berlin. This is not true. Berlin has always underlined its position that first the other division should be here. The operation started because the English relatively quickly withdrew. So we had to stay hard on their heels. The operations were not the intention of Rommel.

The corps chief told me just now that the British in Tobruk have received fresh troops since yesterday. It is very unfortunate that we did not take Tobruk at our first attack, but we have got out of this delicate situation with decency, which is positive. With a little more courage, the English could make us tumble. General Streich is in a mess and his division is no longer organised, because of the fighting. I think that we could make another breakthrough to get into Tobruk if only the Italian troops were somewhat better. Yesterday evening Rommel witnessed an entire Italian regiment abandon its position, as shells fell not even close to them. We were raging. Then they claim to have done everything!

. . .

Four planes bombed us. They dropped a dozen bombs. A vehicle is burning.

. . .

Near Tobruk, 16 April 1941

. . .

Each time we moved quickly forward, the English run away. We have captured an officer and fifteen soldiers. Our losses are low.

Our planes are very active. It could be that we attack again. Yesterday it was extremely hot, guessing between 40° and 45°, but it was still tolerable. We came back dehydrated. We emptied half a dozen cups of tea and two bottles of beer in one gulp.

. . .

19 April 1941

. . .

I have not written to you for two days. I could not do it because I had to lead first an Italian battalion then two German companies to seize a fortification. There were three very hot days with very many losses. I had much luck once again. In Poland and in France, I never survived so many shootings and enemy attacks. I am fine. The operation has been postponed until further notice. Since that night, I am back on the general staff of the Afrika Korps, and for the first time in fifteen days I slept in my tent. I could clean myself after three days. It was great!

Today, I received your dear letters up to 11 April, and in addition two parcels, one with a delicious cake, arriving fresh and well conserved, appreciated by myself and some others who were sitting with me in the mess. Fabulous. A thousand thanks. We all thought the best of you and the others admired your skill at baking. You are the best of all, I cannot help but repeat it.

We are still outside Tobruk. The town is heavily fortified.

Yesterday evening Field Marshal Milch stayed with us. He will send us some aircraft.

6

Outside Tobruk
Letters 19 April–11 July 1941

Near Tobruk, 19 April 1941
Confirm receipt of this letter in particular.
Dearest,
Today, I shall really enjoy Sunday. I already wrote to you this morning, quite early, very briefly, and the courier left; afterwards I cleaned my desk, had breakfast, and now it is 15.30 . . . hopefully there will be no more visitors. But it's like that, if someone arrives to meet one of the staff, he goes first to see the IIa, because he receives all messages.

. . .

After Gazala we moved to the north of Tobruk, near the airfield, but as bombs drop there constantly, the staff has moved over to this place yesterday. It was not very intelligent to move the headquarters to the front, so that you have to be careful not to be hit by bombs and grenades. The command might go into such a dangerous corner for some time, but not the whole staff. The corps chief opposed it, but in this matter Rommel has always other ideas and realises them.

Before arriving here, we spent still a night in Akroma, probably an old Turkish base, in the middle of the desert. So we were moving quite a lot during the last eight days.

Here, we seem to be staying, or rather are forced to stay, as Tobruk, the hole, has not yet fallen. We are already positioned over ten days in front of it. But with existing forces we will not succeed. The individual positions of the English are fortified in such a way that they themselves become modern fortresses, one behind the other, so that we will not succeed with Streich's remaining forces. But I am convinced that if Streich, surprising the enemy at his first attack, had advanced more vigorously, and if he had not had such an inefficient panzer commander, we would not only having been inside Tobruk but even in Alexandria.

But this lack of efficiency influenced the troops. One has, of course, to bear in mind that the troops since Tripoli have been permanently in the desert and having to stand through all these hardships, which one cannot imagine in Germany, so that the troops have strong nerves no longer. But I think that if we have to do something, we should do it and not just stop half way.

That's why everything went on too long before they attacked, and they did not have the nerve, apart from making serious tactical mistakes, to stand it all, especially Olbrich, commander of the panzer regiment. Rommel was already so angry about Streich that I had to formulate a letter to the OKH [supreme command of the army] to replace Streich, likewise Hauser. Only the fact that Streich had his fiftieth birthday the following day made Rommel softer and so he decided to wait for a while. He has already been speaking very seriously with Streich. These days, during which Streich will be completely resting, might bring a change.

The units fighting in places like Sollum and Bardia, because of our situation here, naturally don't have an easy time; they are heavily attacked by the English from the air, by water and by land. Today Rommel has gone there for the first time; the positions will be held by any means. Gradually new troops of the new division will arrive, and then, I think, we will get Tobruk.

But one is not inclined any more to believe that the British will clear off. As it is, their defensive system is so good that they can impose on us heavy fighting with few, but very cleverly positioned, troops.

Two attacks by the Streich division have been completely repulsed, Rommel told me on the 16th, 'You come with me this morning, I will show you the battle ground, two companies of Colonel Knabe's Kr [*Kradschützen*, motorcycle troops] battalion will arrive; you will command them, assuming you take that and the fortress.' First we passed other positions, and in between Rommel was called by Ehlert, informing him that in Bardia, where all kind of things were happening, two companies were needed; Rommel agreed, and he gave me an Italian battalion that was at Akroma instead of the two companies.

Battalion Commander Lieutenant Colonel Bertelli accepted my command and the regiment's commander Colonel de Luca, present, was willing to follow my orders. It took a little while until the battalion was organised in a formation as I wished to have it. Rommel, highly respected by the Italians, had gone in the meantime. Then we advanced nicely, from hill to hill. We cleared hill 204 of English troops, who evacuated it, and I began to dream that I would I come with the Italian battalion up to Tobruk.

But that was wrong. I marched with the front line of the units and the battalion commander followed. As we were about 500 m before Fortress Medannar, we received artillery fire denser than I had ever experienced. The Italians wanted to retreat, I swear; I insulted and threatened them with my pistol, and they did what I told them and began to dig themselves in. But I was not very happy about it, dead Italians around, heavily wounded, screaming with pain, not very encouraging.

But then the firing reduced after an hour and a half; the Italians continued to dig themselves in. As my radio lieutenant as well my interpreter, being next to me, were also wounded, I ran back to tell an Italian motorist to get the radio station, so that I could to report accordingly. The radio station came, and I had hardly written a message when the whole battalion came running back: I shouted and bellowed like a bull and tried to force them to turn, ran forward and saw several English tanks coming, and the first lines of the battalion stopping and raising their hands.

It was hopeless: the closest tank approached more and more wildly shooting at me with his machine gun, I threw myself on the ground and he slowed slightly. I saw the vehicle of the wounded lieutenant close to me, jumped on it: the driver had fled on foot, but he had left the key, I started, and the Italians, I don't know how many, hung on, heaped on the bonnet, so that I could see absolutely nothing while the English tank was shooting, and I rushed wildly driving up to the next hill, where I wanted to stop the running Italians, but in vain.

Then I drove further back, 4 km, driving full of fury. Only there could I stop the first units of the staff and stand firm. The English stopped before us and collected the prisoners. Including the battalion's commander, nearly the entire battalion has gone. That was a surprise! Then the regiment's commander came, moaning about his battalion, from far back with his riding crop, but that type had not even been at the front. Well, it was difficult, with the few people we had, clerks, radio operators and others to occupy the hill.

They always wanted to retreat. The colonel was a coward and anxious. I did not let him go, but he quickly understood and I said only that General Rommel would come. I stayed overnight with the units, but I noticed that all the officers had gone back to Akroma during the night, a distance of 4 km, but they were back in the morning at 4:00 a.m. This cowardly rabble. They left their soldiers behind. Then after 4:00 the wailing began again, I did not let them go.

But then a radio message came from Ehlert saying that Rommel was coming with reinforcements. Well, I didn't worry any more about their wailing. You can't imagine how fast they disappeared, when the first German cars were in sight . . .

But now the two companies who were actually ordered to go to Bardia (it turned out that the situation in Bardia was not so bad) were stopped and ordered to be under my command. I started to instruct the company commanders as Rommel arrived, 'Now off you go, to the front, etc.'

We advanced, but it was not fast enough for him. 'I'll take the right side, you the left.' I agreed, but I felt sorry that my strategy, prepared on my instructions, was foiled, as I knew the terrain. But it got going on Rommel's command, though it did not last as long as the day before, because the English covered us with artillery and machine-gun fire. It became clear that we would not win anything by it.

I fought as I had before when taking part in manoeuvres as a lieutenant; I wanted to get by any means through the wire entanglement. I hoped to succeed with a pioneer unit, but, 30 m before the wire, we were covered with artillery fire and due to losses I no longer had a team to use the anti-tank guns which I had taken along, so I had to stop advancing and to lie where I was.

At another point, I tried with Lieutenant Brinkmann, supposed to be an excellent man with an anti-tank gun, but first Brinkmann's gun was knocked out and then about 50 m before the wire so was mine. I remained in front of it until darkness; it there was no point storming the wire without artillery. Still, I had got further than the day before.

Where Rommel was, I don't know, I didn't see him that evening to speak with him about the losses, because a lot of companies had many losses. I slept in the radio station again and called a meeting of the company chiefs at 4.00 hours to discuss a spearhead attack at five o'clock. The evening before I deliberately said not one word about it because I didn't know what kind of orders I would get for the next day; but the command came that artillery would come the next day. So it was clear that the fortress would be seized.

Only one company chief came to the meeting at 4.00 hours and he did not care about his company. Thus, my plan could not be realised, and I regretted it.

It was clear to me that the day would end without results, but I continued to hope, as Ehlert informed me at 6.00 that around 8.00 Italian artillery and an Italian battalion would arrive.

The artillery was in position and shot excellently; the Italian battalion, a different one than the one two days ago, promptly ran away when the English started to shoot; it was hopeless, especially as the battalion commander fled in fear. Thank God, Rommel arrived at that moment and saw himself that about 800 men running away. The action was off. The Italian artillery shot excellently, but it was senseless to do something without the infantry.

Rommel observed it and called off the attack after having seen the aerial photographs, which I had already viewed in the morning. Even if I had occupied the first fortress, it would have been useless, as the second, third and the fourth were immediately behind. I would not have advanced, as my men would have been killed in the fortification line. So I just organised several heavy weapons to the front; we were shelled, but then I called off the action.

Moreover, English aircraft arrived with bombs, low-flying aircraft with machine guns; it was hard at times. Then I was informed about an order from the general that I would be replaced by another major, coming in the evening to command the company that would become the reserve. I was a little bit sad to leave the company, but when I learned that it would become the reserve, I agreed.

The English had complete air superiority. Four English aircraft were over us, a reconnaissance aircraft and three bombers; they showed the English artillery individual spots, and then we were covered by the artillery fire, so we did not believe we could come out unhurt. It was a horrible feeling to lie there helplessly, with no anti-aircraft units. The outcome of General Field Marshal Milch's visit yesterday to this morning was that now three fighters came over from Sicily, to shoot down three English bombers soon. These most miserable moments of bombing will hopefully stop. A group of fighters will come over, and then the English will suffer.

. . .

We have had a lot of losses from artillery shelling. In the evening at

21.00 I was back at the corps staff, where they suspected me having been captured. This was because my driver, having seen at a distance of 500 metres for a short moment before he ran away that the Italians were fleeing with their arms in the air, saw that I was running to the Italians to stop them, so they thought that I was captured along with them.

. . .

Well, at least these were days full of events with rich experiences. And I was happy at having been once again at the front, though it is, of course, nicer to do it with your own company. Rommel and the corps chief have very much appreciated my way of handling the situation. They have seen that I have tried everything, but nothing could be done. Only for you: this outcome was caused by Rommel's error, as the photos had probably been here for days. One should have realised that such an attack on Tobruk could only have been done after careful preparation and planning.

[The end is missing]

Near Tobruk, 20 April 1941

. . .

English aircraft have again bombed us during the night, this morning twice already. I think and hope that this will stop soon, if some are shot down every day. Each time, it is an unpleasant feeling. Rommel and the corps chief only came back this morning. On the way back, they were attacked by English low-flying aircraft. Rommel's driver and another died, a third was wounded. Maybe Rommel finally takes it as a further sign that he had been lucky again. His place is not at the front. The situation at Sollum and Bardia is satisfying despite the English attacks.

. . .

It is difficult to understand the English. Have they been reinforced in Tobruk or not? Nevertheless, we have to wait for the arrival of parts of the new division before we start attacking Tobruk again. The division of General Streich has so far lost around a thousand men, dead or captured, mostly in the battle for Tobruk.

You can take it from me that my appointment as adjutant of the Afrika Korps was an award. Rommel's character is above reproach. I definitely know this well, because I discuss personnel items with him and work on them.

In the *Reich* an article about Rommel has appeared, a pompous article giving false information. Rommel's father was not handyman, but grammar school director; he himself had never been a leader of the SA [*Sturmabteilung*, Storm Division, a combat force of the national-socialist party]. We will protest against the publication.

. . .

Near Tobruk, 21 April 1941

. . .

Five minutes ago, Rommel's aide, Aldinger, came and gave me from Rommel four chocolate bars, six oranges and nuts in chocolate. It was a gift from the commander of the squadron. He gave something to the corps chief and to me. That's nice of him.

A company of captured English soldiers arrived, who landed at Bardia. It does not look at all like the English want to abandon Tobruk. Rommel is thinking of requesting additional troops.

. . .

Near Tobruk, 22 April 1941

. . .

We have not yet changed our position. In the evening again some bombs, one of them next to Rommel's car. Nothing happened. A second in front of the field kitchen, a dud. The bombs are smaller now. Because of the presence of our own interceptor fighters the English aircraft have to fly very high and had to reduce the bomb load. The topic of yesterday's division meeting was the decision to occupy Tobruk at a later date.

Over the next ten days, your cousin Wim will arrive here. Hopefully, the steamer will not be sunk as has happened to some in recent times. Soldiers are generally rescued, but the war material, which is urgently needed, is missing.

Yesterday evening, I buried Rommel's two drivers at a nice spot on the big road at kilometre stone 31. The place will be arranged properly later.

The situation has become quite critical in the meantime. The English have attacked us. If we only had two more German divisions here, we could have been in Cairo for days. Currently, the situation seems to have calmed somewhat. There are always excitements.

. . .

23 April 1941

. . .

After the English having attacked again yesterday evening, we thought that they would bother us again on the early morning. But nothing happened. I myself got up shortly after 4.00 to control the guards. Now we believe again that the English might give up Tobruk. With the existing German forces and the military failure of the Italians, we cannot do very much. This nest, Tobruk, is strongly fortified that it cannot be taken for the moment. Still waiting.

On this occasion I realise that I wanted to tell you the reason why I do not constantly accompany the general. It is the fact that we transferred Aldinger to Rommel as his personal aide. In fact, I should constantly accompany Rommel, but this solution is a thousand times better, because I can do my office work. If I wish to accompany him, I can still do it any time. Moreover, Rommel is obviously very much concerned that nothing should happen to me. He cannot prevent it, because in wars especially with existing superiority in the air and strong artillery fire you are nowhere secure.

. . .

Sometimes the question arises whether we are ending the war here in summer or not. However, I believe that it will continue here until the goal is reached. I still reckon that we will be in Cairo no later than the end of May.

Yesterday evening, this morning already for half an hour and now again at least for one hour, I have been chatting with the corps chief. If he has time, he always comes to see me. He is very nice, and we are on very good terms.

. . .

24 April 1941

Yesterday evening the corps chief asked me to come over in his command car. However, our get-together was affected by the message that suddenly sixty British tanks were spotted at Bardia driving to the west. We couldn't work out where they suddenly came from in such strength. The situation over there as here is tense this morning. We were informed that there were enemy advances at different places, which had all been warded off by 9.00. Yesterday we still had the impression that the English might clear out of the place.

I just met Rommel. It is quite difficult for him. Only a person with strong nerves, like him, can cope with this situation. This morning, another Italian company surrendered. It is a shame that we have not got enough German troops here.

I just heard that the attack of the sixty tanks was driven off. The rest will be done by aircraft. The English artillery is shooting again more than before; the English aircraft were active overnight.

. . .

25 April 1941

. . .

The night was quiet, even this morning. It is rare. One is sitting on a powder keg. We know nothing about the English. It also looks as if Berlin will not send us further reinforcements. North Africa could become a theatre of secondary importance. Otherwise it is incomprehensible to me. Berlin should know what is needed. Rommel is not very happy about this imposed pause.

If we had taken Tobruk, it would be certainly different, and also more satisfying. The English are so disciplined in the military field that they let our troops advance so as to shoot them at the last moment.

. . .

26 April 1941

. . .

I had the intention to visit all regiments for a few days to get to know the officer's corps. This does not to seem to be very useful, since the losses cause constant changes. Yesterday afternoon Gariboldi came to see Rommel, who reproached him the bad military behaviour of his soldiers.

Rommel is preparing a plan for a new assault on Tobruk. Nevertheless, I suppose that we still have ten days more in this canyon.

After a lengthy consultation with Rommel and the corps chief, both have been given orders that I should be proposed for an Italian decoration, the silver medal of bravery.

. . .

27 April 1941

. . .

I have asked Rommel for a new military mission. He said no: 'I have already worried about you once. I do understand, but you are irreplaceable for me.' . . .

28 April 1941

. . .

I would like to go once more to Derna to the sea, a town full of roses and carnations. One has such a deep desire to see something beautiful, something pure. It is for far too long that we have lived in this dirt. And it seems increasingly unlikely that we will come out of it. But we are not impatient; we are all right. We have food and drink.

About the outcome of the meetings in Berlin, I cannot yet tell you anything. But I imagine that Rommel was ordered to be patient, in order not to experience disaster by any premature act. The transport of supply, food, ammunition and spare parts is still not yet assured, so we still can't access the actual frontline. Malta probably has to be occupied first, as we cannot leave the English at our flank.

. . .

29 April 1941

. . .

Cooperation with our Italian allies is too difficult. Everything has to be considered down to the smallest detail and to be harmonised.

The situation has hardly changed. The English are remarkably calm. Last night they shot parachute flares right in our direction, but the night was calm. Ship guns shot again in our direction. Then again above us an English plane at 4:00.

If you get these lines, there are now four more weeks since we saw each other last. Add another three more months, and our reunion will certainly be not too far away. Who will hunt the roe this year in Klein Silkow?

. . .

30 April 1941

. . .

With our squadron, stationed at a beautiful sandy beach, it was especially nice. It is clear that the men have a particularly agreeable, comradely relationship with each other.

Tonight the great moment: the assault on Tobruk. Maybe you will get a special announcement about its occupation. It would be nice if the place were finally in our hands, so that the previous losses were not in vain.

Just now, a daring English Hurricane was above us, perhaps only 100 metres up, covering the area with machine-gun fire. This is the first fire from English aircraft for days . . .

Of Tobruk not much should be left. But it is surprising that ships are still operating in the port. It is said that many of them have gone aground.
. . .

Near Tobruk, 1 May 1941

. . .

The attack began at the fortification line of Tobruk at 18.00. First the Stukas attacked, and then the artillery shot until approximately 21:00 with all its barrels, less overnight, and this morning at four o'clock it started anew. The beginning was quite satisfactory, and could also . . . [deleted by the censor] . . . This morning, it became clear that the target had not been reached everywhere.

The English fight: tough, brave, but also mean. At one place someone had shouted to the Germans at night in German: 'Do not shoot, here are Germans.' When our soldiers approached, he shot them.

I spent two hours with Rommel. The result of the assault was not satisfactory. The English artillery shoots perfectly, so that a planned advance is not possible. The units are regrouped now to attack again in the evening, when the heat is over. I think . . . [three more passages blacked out by the censor].

When the Stukas come, the English go into their bunkers. They come about three times a day. I observed an air battle close by, three English aircraft against two German fighters: the German fighters were great. One supported the other, so they shot an English plane down. The pilot jumped with a parachute, then the machine span and then fell straight to the ground and burned. I never observed an air battle so well. The German fighters are dynamic, agile and bold. One of them places himself behind the enemy and shoots at him, while the second covers it.

According to estimates we caught 300 English as prisoners, but our losses were important, as we heard. Appel, commanding an Italian unity since yesterday evening, unfortunately had a nervous breakdown; he was probably angered by the Italians, and also the effects of the shooting and fighting. It is not so easy here in Africa, certainly substantially more difficult here than at other theatres.

I still continue to suppose that we shall get Tobruk and won't have to retreat. But with the given forces, it is obviously not possible to realise our objective.

Still outside Tobruk, 2 May 1941

. . .

We could advance in some places more than 3 km, at other positions not at all. We could continue moving further with the few German forces we have. To anyone who knows this difficult ground, which is filled with ramparts defended by tough English soldiers, it was a remarkable success. This relative success unfortunately caused considerable losses. In the evening twenty English tanks turned up, but were driven off. Rommel will now, at 7.oo, go to the front again. So it might be that according to his impression our position will be somewhat improved, but generally real progress cannot yet be seen. How long we shall have to wait, I cannot tell you. With the Italians nothing can be achieved, if they just desert. Yesterday many cars filled up with Italian soldiers were seen retreating; when they were stopped they could show had neither reason nor warrant.

. . .

I just talked with Rommel. He is always full of optimism. Colonel Knabe, having come from Sollum with his unit, has again distinguished himself by storming several shelters. So I submitted him by radio for the Knight's Cross, likewise Major Voigtsberger and Lieutenant Wolff, who had pulverised seven tanks. I hope that their performances, which are much higher up the scale than during the campaign in France, will be realised in Berlin.

In short, dearest, I am fine, but the overall situation could be better, but there is nothing to do. I hope that the English won't find out about our weakness.

. . .

Still near Tobruk, 3 May 1941

. . .

Thunder and lightning everywhere. If you don't witness it yourself, you can hardly imagine it. Although I have already seen quite a number of shellings, the one tonight is particularly good.

This morning I accompanied General Rommel from 7.00 hours onwards. Especially interesting were the bunkers of the English which were stormed yesterday. They are barely visible. They are cleverly dug into the ground and well camouflaged.

It is quite understandable now why our aircraft could not discover them. I myself thought they were ridiculous piles of rocks. The English dominate the entire area with them. The shelters are integrated about 4 m deep in the ground. They are concrete and withstand each air attack by the Stukas, especially by the artillery. I now feel sorry for all my men who died. There was no chance of success against these fortifications.

If we succeed in getting Tobruk this time, then it will be a great merit for the General, because the attack did not start at dawn but was delayed to the evening. No sooner did I start to write this letter than Rommel's aide, Aldinger, came in with a bottle of white wine from Rommel.

Today I met Lieutenant Colonel Knabe. He looks well and is sunburnt; he looks as well as I have ever seen him. He is happy, the real front soldier. Quite apart from his military merits, he offers, through his analysis, his optimism and his temerity, the image of an example commander.

I currently have no cars to give. Total losses are on the agenda. The best cars don't stand long journeys on this difficult terrain.

At a consultation with Rommel, he gave me a pile of letters to answer. Many people want to have his photo with his autograph.

If the Italian officers were more courageous, their troops would be pretty good. They are always delighted when they see German officers welcoming us with '*camerada*'. Their soldiers, extremely helpful, love to be commanded. If there no leadership and no model, the result cannot be good. For us, this is not enough. We require proper training, education and a sense of duty.

. . .

5 May 1941

. . .

We talked about politics after the Führer's speech before the Reichstag, which we could hear quite clearly. I was extremely disappointed. I expected something positive. I thought that the Führer could tell us now

My parents on the day of their wedding, 29 September 1931.

Near the mosque in Benghazi, an armoured vehicle has been taken by storm by the population. 'Comrades described the great joy of the inhabitants of Benghazi when we were marching in.' (page 76)

Panzers and other armoured vehicles enter Tripoli, March 1941. (page 62)

General Rommel with my father overlooking the plain of Benghazi. The city is located on the northern coast of Libya.

My father in front of his tent.

Parade at Tripoli (1 and 2 March 1941): Gariboldi, Italian Commander-in-Chief, and General Rommel were greeted by 'huge and enthusiastic crowds'. (page 58)

Military review at Tripoli to mark Rommel's appointment. (20 February 1941)

Members of the Afrika Korps infantry move into position prior to the attack on Marsa Brega, which started on 31 March 1941 (page 74).

Tanks of the Panzer Regiment 5 race towards Tobruk in April 1941. (page 79)

Aerial view of Fort Acroma, 30 km west of Tobruk. (page 120)

Erwin Rommel, Commander of the Afrika Korps.

From left to right: my father, Colonel Heggenreiner, Italian troops' liaison officer, Gariboldi, Italian Commander-in-Chief, and General Rommel. 'Some have whispered mockingly that Rommel would have preferred to see the ruins of which he himself was responsible . . .' (page 102)

A German officer mingles with the crowd in Benghazi.

Rommel and two of his closest colleagues: Colonel von dem Borne, chief of staff of the Afrika Korps (left), and General Fröhlich, Luftwaffe (right).

Artillery in position before Tobruk, in June 1941.

Searchlights scanning the night sky for British aircraft at Tripoli. (page 63)

Rommel's visit to Hauptmann Wilhelm Bach and his men after the Battle of Sollum, 18 June 1941 (page 120). In civilian life, Bach was a pastor.

Hauptmann Bach stands to the left of Rommel. Schraepler thought that Bach, nicknamed the 'Pastor in Purgatory', was 'likely to become the first clergyman to receive the Knight's Cross'. He was awarded this honour on 9 July 1941.

After the Battle of Sollum: a group of soldiers examines the burnt-out British tank 'Matilda'. (page 120)

Rommel's visit to Italian officers and artillerymen at 'the famous, strategically important' Halfaya Pass after the Battle of Sollum. (page 120)

British prisoners are rounded up in the vicinity of Fort Acroma. (page 120)

Near the mosque of Bardia: Rommel (back view) in conversation with his staff officers, including Major Wüstefeld and my father. (page 122)

Rommel inspecting the Sollum sector: a stop on the road overlooking the Gulf of Sollum.

Rommel's visit to Italian artillerymen at Halfaya Pass after the Battle of Sollum. Rommel, General von Ravenstein and Italian officers take stock on the map.

Rommel acclaimed by Italian artillerymen after the battle of Sollum.

'Three days ago, I was slightly injured. A piece of shrapnel hit my right temple. I am fine. I have no complaints.' During the retreat of the Panzergruppe Afrika in November and December 1941 my father was wounded (page 182). This is the last photograph taken of my father.

December 1941 was a black month for Panzergruppe Afrika. Here we see the graves of General Max Sümmermann, of my father, and of General Walter Neumann-Silkow, my mother's cousin, at Derna Cemetery. (page 188)

that we would be home at Christmas. But it became clear that the war will go for a very long time. This message had apparently no remnant of the hope that was in his New Year's message. I noticed that neither Russia, nor Turkey, nor America were mentioned. But our technical reception was not so good that one could hear all the nuances. Maybe you know better. Pistorius is silent or only cautious.

. . .

Although Rommel had promised not to go to the front line any more as he did yesterday, he did it again. And again he was fired at. When he came back, he did not seem to be very happy. He just said, 'Our boys are tired.' They should all be replaced once. Again and again to be in this dirt, in the heat and under permanent shelling (in one minute, 80 to 86 shots), not even the strongest nerves could stand it. All this, they have to bear everything. None of our fronts demand so much of our soldiers; even if the Führer was saying said that the war in the Balkans was so far the hardest. At least there was plenty of water, but here there is a shortage of everything. Even the way of fighting is different. We have had more losses so far, unfortunately much more than all divisions put together over there. These losses should certainly not play an important role in assessing the war, but they remain an indication of the seriousness of the fighting.

. . .

6 May 1941

. . .

In the meantime, Rommel has received instructions, approved by the Führer, no longer to engage in a large-scale assault on Tobruk. Smaller attacks could be carried out. Cairo remains in reserve for peace. Nevertheless, I still hope that we will one day take Tobruk. Last night we won another hill. The English had evacuated it in time. Our position is slowly improving. For the soldiers who have just come from Europe and are immediately sent to the front in the desert, it is particularly difficult.

Yesterday Gariboldi came to see Rommel to inform him that the highest military award had been conferred on him.

7 May 1941

. . .

The night was calm again. Rommel has given me another pile of his incoming mail: some 200 letters from men and women, boys and girls, members of the Hitler Youth. Everybody wants to get an autograph or a photo. So I have suggested that Rommel gets himself photographed. Some letters are pretty funny, especially those of the girls, using an oft-chosen phrase, 'to our brave boys'. The wife of a forest warden near Aachen sent a book of Goethe's letters! Not ideal for the General!

I wonder if you received the letter I wrote yesterday. I crossed out a paragraph, as if to say to the censor, in case they open my mail and call me to account: 'I crossed it out, so it's not valid, just a personal opinion.' Just so you know.

8 May 1941

. . .

Despite the moonlight, last night was calm. Everybody welcomed the break. We lack ammunition. There are enormous difficulties with supplies. Sometimes this is missing, sometimes that. We always lack loading capacity. A large quantity of supplies has arrived in Tripoli, but we could not transport it.

Lately, the Arabs have refused to unload ships, because some time ago, planes bombed and killed some of their compatriots, and sent the vessel to the bottom of the harbour.

Tripoli is regularly bombed and the entrance to its port mined. Several units have arrived without vehicles but cannot be transported to the front. This explains why we have a lot of problems in the field of supplies.

. . .

9 May 1941

. . .

Yesterday the *ghibli* blew all day and only stopped at three o'clock. There was terrible dirt everywhere; it got into the nose, was simply everywhere. The flapping of the canvas tent was an insupportable noise.

At Tobruk, it was more or less calm, although artillery fired back a lot. We all unimpressed by these shellings now.

Yesterday evening, the daily *Skat* with the corps chief was disrupted by constant calls: the English attacked Sollum.

Very disturbing are the important losses of ships, which we are currently suffering. The English have once again sunk a steamer before

Benghazi. It would indeed be extremely unfortunate and not good if we were to fold because ammunition and food are no longer arriving. No coastal steamer seems to come through. Either the English are on the lookout, or they have laid mines. We depend on these vessels because we do not have enough cargo capacity and gasoline for road transport from Tripoli to go up to here (1,600 km).

Transport by road is time consuming and costs material. In addition, there are losses of ships while crossing between Italy and Tripoli, and into the port of Tripoli. The Italians don't do anything. They have no planes and no fleet to fight in the Mediterranean. It is depressing. But, dearest, when you receive this letter, the matter will be different again. The Englishman is a cool calculator. He knows that he can leave us in peace at the front, when cutting supplies behind. Berlin has no idea of these problems.

We have been here for a quarter of a year, the corps chief and I. It is depressing to see how the time passes. What will bring us the next quarter? Returning home? Certainly not yet. For us here, there are still only heat and dirt.

. . .

11 May 1941

. . .

Almost all day, I wrote letters for Rommel, or I dictated them. He receives more and more letters. Yesterday, a young girl wrote that she would like to get to know an African! A shoemaker in Berlin would like to exercise his profession here. Members of the Hitler Youth want a photo.

The night was calm again. It seems that the English are preparing a larger operation at Sollum on 13 May. But they will be surprised, because we have strengthened our presence there. Skirmishes are everywhere on the agenda. Apparently, the English want to keep Tobruk at all costs. Taking Crete would relieve us very much. At present, we transport everything by road. That is not very much; enough, I hope, not to have to retreat for lack of supplies. That would be a battle won by the English.

. . .

It seems to me, however, that we have become secondary theatre for Berlin. The English must have a huge stock of ammunition at their disposal. It is unimaginable, the amount of shells that they have used up in recent weeks. When they retreated from Tobruk, the Italians did not raze their own artillery and large ammunition depots. Therefore the English shoot with the materiel left. It is unfortunate that we pay for this stupid negligence. The English have once again bombed our positions overnight. It was bright as daylight. Yesterday evening, I spent an hour chatting with Rommel.

I am fine. I wouldn't have believed before that heat would have such little effect on me. But if we can already stand 62°C, we will also stand 72°. Rather, we think now of the rainy season in winter, hoping to be back in time for Christmas.

. . .

12 May 1941

. . .

Yesterday, at 11 a.m., Excellency Gariboldi came to award to Rommel the Cross of Commander of the Order of Savoy. I positioned two tanks on either side of the two men. On the left the Italians, the Germans on the right; it offered a good view of the ceremony to the cameramen and photographers. It will certainly be in the news. You can see me right behind Rommel. Gariboldi mentioned first General von Prittwitz, killed in action. Lunch was served after a meeting between Rommel and Gariboldi.

I recently sent a car to Sollum, where some British stocks are still stored in a truck including canned food. I could offer an excellent soup with vegetables, which everybody liked. Mineral water and red wine, coffee afterwards.

At 14.00 hours, Gariboldi wanted to go to the front. For the Italians stationed there, it will be a good thing.

According to information coming in, the British fleet will come in our direction, so we thought we would be harassed overnight. But nothing happened apart from some firing. Now we are curious to learn what the reconnaissance flight found out. The English must be somewhere.

13 May 1941

. . .

Another girl wrote Rommel that she would like to get to know a soldier with sensitive feelings. A member of the Hitler Youth wrote: 'Dear General, I would like to make the acquaintance of an unknown soldier.

That is why I am writing to you.'

We are still not yet very clear what the English really intend. They seem to be quite strong in Tobruk, but probably not yet in Egypt. We continue to believe that we could make a breakthrough without difficulty to Cairo, as long as we are sufficiently supplied with men and equipment. Berlin will be perhaps using his right of veto as we don't know the overall situation either, nor we can assess it. We fervently hope that Crete will soon be occupied by our troops, which would be a great help.

We believe it impossible that the war will end this year. It is also possible that we'll only allowed to move towards Egypt in the autumn. Thus the most curious assumptions are circulating in our discussions.

14 May 1941

Dearest, in haste, as I go with Rommel to Cyrene to meet His Excellence Gariboldi.

. . .

15 May 1941

My beloved, I was unable to continue yesterday. Rommel informed me by his aide that he would be putting on his best uniform. I also had to change and I was not even able to write a few words.

The journey to Cyrene with a stop-over at Derna was interesting. The landscape disappointed me. Human settlements were separated by large distances; there were herds of goats and sheep, cows, occasionally a horse, herds of camels, dreary fields, but beautiful vineyards. When you come from the desert, you welcome every green leaf. On top of the mountains we had a wonderful view on several bays, and especially on the blue-green-coloured sea. The hotel where Gariboldi resides is located in the most beautiful part of Cyrene. Romans, Greeks, Egyptians, Turks and now the Italians quickly discovered the most scenic spots of Cyrene.

Rommel decorated Gariboldi the Iron Cross, First and Second Class, in the beautiful lobby in presence of the officers' corps. He was pleased and visibly moved. The two generals had lunch in a small dining room and I joined the Italian officers in the great hall. For them, it was their regular menu offered for lunch and dinner, but not since Tripoli had I eaten so well: macaroni with tomato puree and grated cheese, pâté with potatoes, followed by cheese, coffee, red and white wines, cognac. Italians here are not aware of the war and believe that they pay over the top for their food to get good quality.

Gariboldi showed us the temple of Zeus and the ruins. He himself served as a guide. Some have whispered mockingly that Rommel would have preferred to see the ruins of which he himself was responsible . . . but I think that this day was also for him a pleasant trip. We have just received bad news coming from Sollum. I cannot believe that so many English tanks can turn up so suddenly without being detected.

. . .

16 May 1941

. . .

When you receive this letter, you will know already that the English attacked us by surprise at Sollum. We were forced to retreat. They still hold Sollum. Fighting continues around Fort Capuzzo. The numerical superiority of the English tanks made our position to be untenable, although the ground favoured us. The English are supposed to have taken fifty prisoners, we seventy. The situation is serious and continues to be so. It looks like a large-scale attack to reduce the pressure on Tobruk.

. . .

Nevertheless, we tried a breakthrough on Tobruk. At one spot, we took three forts, at another two. It seems that the English, to save their prestige, felt compelled to undertake a counter-attack, which explains the attack on Sollum. The taking of Crete will take place, we believe, in the near future, followed by the advance of our troops to Syria and Iraq. We will have eventful days ahead. I have no news from Knabe; he is involved in the fighting around Sollum, but he is certainly fine.

Needless to comment on Rudolf Hess's flight to England. When you receive this letter, dear, everything will have significantly changed. The English will consider Hess mad, so he will not harm anyone. They could just as well say that our political leaders are all mad. It is surprising how little attention the English news pay to it. They probably really do think he's mad.

. . .

16 May 1941

. . .

This morning, the Chief of Staff ordered me to find a new location for the headquarters. But 50 km to our rear! As a measure of precaution. I found a gorgeous canyon close to the sea.

The fighting around Sollum continued today with varying luck, though Sollum and Fort Capuzzo fell back into our hands. In the end we had more solid nerves than the English, although they were far superior. Knabe won back Capuzzo. Our soldiers have fought with morale of steel. Although the English retreated at the end of the day, it is feared that the battle will continue tomorrow, in view of their superiority. The fighting in the desert is really particularly bitter. We don't think anybody at home can imagine it.

. . .

My tent seems to be a meeting point, with comings and goings. Most discussions are about the situation and show concern. My visitors, drinking a cup of coffee or a glass of red wine, want to unwind mentally and psychologically. Under these circumstances, I can no longer do my office work. I think that the situation at the front will calm down tomorrow. Unfortunately, I am aware that my prognoses do not always come true!

Today, General von Esebeck, successor of Major General von Prittwitz und Gaffron, was injured during an air raid at low altitude.

. . .

18 May 1941

. . .

Yesterday it was generally calm. Sollum is back in our hands. A British armoured attack was repulsed: twenty-five prisoners.

Yesterday, Gariboldi came to award the Chief of Staff with the Knight's Cross of Savoy. A nice little decoration. Rommel awarded the Iron Cross, Second Class, to an Italian division commander and to other Italian officers. During a special ceremony, he awarded the Iron Cross, First and Second class, posthumously to Major Frongia, an officer of great merit, who died of a serious wound yesterday. We were sad that this good and decent man were no longer here to enjoy the decoration. As Rommel could not attend his burial, I accompanied Gariboldi in his place.

. . .

19 May 1941

. . .

The front does not calm down. My opinion, probably only wishful thinking, that the English would withdraw from here after the taking of Crete, was not accepted neither by Rommel nor the Chief of Staff. They think rather that the English will renew operations such as the attack of Sollum. We shall be more careful now. We had hoped that Crete would be taken yesterday, but the concentration of the British fleet at its west coast has thwarted our operation.

. . .

Yesterday, I wrote and dictated a vast amount of letters on the general's behalf, and sent the new photos which were well done. I am afraid that not hundreds but thousands will ask for a photo. This is the price of glory. As seen, it is of no use, to become a famous man.

Esebeck's successor, the future general of the 15th Armoured Division, has not yet arrived. We suffer daily from heavy losses, often caused by stone splinters that lead to dangerous injuries.

20 May 1941

My beloved, yesterday we had another quiet day, the night likewise, at least for us. At the front intensive fighting and reconnaissance patrols continue.

Wim visited me yesterday. A surprise! He has become a true front soldier, having already seen a lot. Last night, he returned to his position, as he will be better protected in the shelters than in the vast desert, where men are exposed to shells and bombs. He suffered an attack from an aircraft at low altitude. He told me that it was frightening.

The English have by far still the supremacy of the air. When will Crete finally fall to relieve us? I just saw Rommel to sign documents. He told me that the time had come for us to install in a canyon by the seaside, with the opportunity to swim.

The situation in Sollum is again calm. The preparations for a positional warfare are in full swing. Trenches, etc. I cannot write about it in detail. They were used before, during World War I, but not so far this time. They are constructed in an exemplary manner.

Yesterday and the day before yesterday, we recorded temperatures of around 60°C. We had a long debate. I am persuaded that I have to accept the temperature where I live. In Germany, the situation would be quite different; I could avoid the heat by going into the shade.

We drink several litres per day. Currently, we have enough water. Yesterday, I inspected the tents for water cans. I discovered something surprising. Quite a number of comrades have hoarded water. In one tent we found eight cans of water (20 litres each). This is not very comradely, because everyone is entitled only to 5 litres. I drank all mine yesterday.

. . .

I intend to write to the personnel office, to send a copy of a battle report. It shows that a lieutenant and a commander of a tank unit have completely failed in battle again. I want them to understand that it is not our fault, if they decide to take them to court martial. An explanation is necessary because of the huge demands asked of us all. I feel compelled to do it also out of respect for others.

. . .

21 May 1941

. . .

This morning, at 7 a.m., I left with Rommel to inspect the location that I have chosen for the staff. I almost did not find the canyon, which would have been a problem. Rommel was in a particularly execrable humour today. In addition, he did not have much time. I found the gorge at the last minute! In the desert, there are scarcely signs to guide you. He accepted my choice immediately. Tomorrow we shall move. At this new location, we shall always have a breeze to refresh us, in addition to it sun and water, even if it is very salty, but no sirocco and no dust. It's beautiful, provided that the English don't raid us by the sea.

. . .

Our troops will take Crete in the next few days. Then Cyprus. If we were at the Suez Canal, we would have encircled the English. It was so hot yesterday that I drank all my litres of water. Everything we all drink, including tea and coffee, is accounted in our litre allowance. The consequence: this morning I had no water left for washing.

Rommel gave instructions to court-martial the two officers: the commander of an armoured unit and a lieutenant. This measure causes great concern within the armoured units. The captain and one of our best officers in prison! I don't know what is happening here at the moment.

The heat seems to affect everybody. We should certainly take steps to avoid further problems. The tropical heat and other inconveniences is making a lot of soldiers nervous. What each member of the Afrika Korps has to accept here in Africa is enormous. Personally, I feel excellent.

22 May 1941

. . .

This morning, we moved. The displacement has caused fewer problems than I thought. Everywhere members of the staff are working in front of their tents, digging and camouflaging their tents against the enemy. The sections of the staff can work again. Vehicles and a second part of the staff are positioned in a dried up wadi, relatively well protected.

Rommel had picked a good spot for the corps chief. But he, when he got there and found out that my tent had been put up somewhere else, placed his command car near me: 'I'll have to keep an eye on you!' Our discussions and analysis of the situation will not be interrupted by the move. For security reasons, facilities and tents are more dispersed than usual. In peacetime, we would pay a fortune for a stay on such a beautiful beach in Africa.

. . .

If there was no firing in the distance since 4 a.m., we could forget about the war, nestled in the canyon close to the sea. But how can we not think about our poor comrades buried in a hole unable to move, subjected to continued gunfire in the heat and shivering in the cold at night? It's only at night that they can take turns to get their food for the next twenty-four hours. Really, it is not easy!

My beloved, you in Germany should not lose your patience. You should only think that we will come back one day. And then, and then we will have formidable moments together.

. . .

24 May 24 1941

. . .

Scores of soldiers are sick. This number is increasing every day.

. . .

24 May 1941

. . .

Yesterday morning, close to my beach an English life-jacket floated ashore; today, a big plank of wood was found nearby. Thus, in the early morning, one is reminded that many destinies are finished off at sea.

To our great sorrow, two company commanders were killed in action. While the sirocco was blowing yesterday, they went the wrong way.

But who knows what's going to happen here! The situation does not give the impression that the war will end, but rather become a permanent state of affairs. We are still awaiting the occupation of Crete. The English news doesn't provide a clear picture.

. . .

25 May 1941

. . .

Yesterday, the announcement of the occupation of the western part of Crete was quite nice. The capitulation of the entire island will be just a question of several days. Yesterday, we had the impression that the English would withdraw from Tobruk. But this morning, our interpretation was quite different.

We learned that hundreds and hundreds of kilos [of parcels] are stuck in Tripoli, and likewise hundreds and hundreds of kilos of private mail in Naples. Means of transport are lacking. It is more important to use the holds of ships for the transport of ammunition and food than for parcels! We are all right, not too bad at all. Packages represent only a pleasant extra. For instance, I am fighting with the Chief of Staff, so far unsuccessfully, for replacement battalions to be transported here. 'Supply is not yet assured,' he answered me. If these battalions could be here to renew the quota, leave could more easily be organised. Currently, it is impossible. Hence soldiers are serving their full time at the front.

. . .

26 May 1941 (Sunday)

. . .

My beloved, Sunday passed faster than I hoped in the morning. On holidays and on Sundays time elapses in the same manner as other days. Pfistermeister prepared fried eggs at noon, so that tells us it's Sunday today. Lieutenant Wagner has put on a white shirt. Everyone tries to interpret the Sunday in his own way.

This afternoon several squadrons of our planes overflew our position. We know that they sank four freighters before Tobruk. Rommel continues to think that the English will abandon Tobruk. That would be so good we don't want to think of it!

Our intelligence service have not observed English units any longer outside Sollum. A commando will be sent today to verify the situation.

Already the occupation of the western part of Crete is having a positive impact for us. For several days, we have not heard any more English planes, nor received shells fired by the Royal Navy. Yesterday, Rommel received a message from the supreme command in Berlin, signed by von Brauchitsch, criticising his reports. There is no doubt that the situation here has been very serious. It is only thanks to Rommel's activities and some very capable officers that we have consolidated our position again.

Yesterday, at noon, a mine was washed up on our beach. It was blown up. The power of the detonation was impressive. I hope you get my letters regularly so that you do not need to be sad. Think always that I am fine and that I am having summer holidays.

. . .

28 May 1941

. . .

Yesterday evening, at nightfall, the English tried a break-out of Tobruk near the main road, and again this morning. Both attacks were repulsed.

The operation near Sollum was successful: 62 prisoners, 7 heavy tanks, the famous Mark II, 2 light tanks and 9 cannons.

. . .

You will be surprised to learn who is transferred here: your cousin, Walter Neumann-Silkow, to command the 15th Armoured Division during the absence of General von Esebeck.

Today, we expect the announcement that Crete is taken. When will America enter the war? It is probably only a matter of days. If they do, this war will be very long. I hope that you in Germany will not suffer too much from the consequences.

The Mediterranean will soon be cleansed of the English. What will they do with their troops stationed in Abyssinia? At this time, a great number of relevant questions is coming up. What are our political choices concerning Russia?

. . .

30 May 1941

. . .

The Chief of Staff has left for Germany via Tripoli, as planned. He could have flown directly to Rome, but English fighters still dominate the air. He is entrusted with many important special missions and interviews of great importance for us.

After shooting all day, the night was almost calm. Fifty to sixty aircraft of our air force have overflown us twice at low altitude. They sank two British ships before Tobruk. The English continue to strengthen their fortifications overnight.

. . .

30 May, 1941

. . .

You worry a lot about politics. We talk about it very little. However, it concerns us to a great extent.

You ask after Graf Baudissin. Like my old interpreter, Dr Littner, he was taken prisoner by the English. Both are in Cairo.

. . .

31 May 1941

. . .

Right out of my tent this morning, I saw a cargo ship on the horizon. We alerted our planes. The ship began to shoot at them; they responded by dropping three bombs. The freighter caught fire, and then we saw a speedy motorboat leaving it. After some dazzling blazes, a detonation, more powerful than I had ever heard. A huge dark cloud rose, everything was over, the freighter was gone. Obviously an ammunition carrier.

Yesterday, Major Appel called on me to say goodbye. After a brief stay here, this man is seriously ill. All his limbs were shaking and he is suffering from psychological confusion. Apart from problems with his nerves, he suffers from a brain concussion. Even if his health improves, we shall not see him here again. There is no reason to send elderly people here.

1 June 1941

. . .

The freighter yesterday came from Alexandria was filled with water and ammunition. He had escaped three air raids and had not found the entrance to the port of Tobruk. His crew consisted of fourteen people: four Greeks and ten English. Two of them were seriously injured. One died shortly thereafter. The entrance to the harbour of Tobruk is blocked by sunken ships.

The war will continue probably for a long time. First, we will have to conquer the whole of Africa, and finally Cape Town as well. This is one way to learn about the whole continent.

You will certainly be in Klein Silkow from the end of June to mid-August? I shall probably go on leave at the end of August. But I have to coordinate my leave with Rommel. I am one of the staff who has stayed here the longest, without interruption.

. . .

2 June 1941

. . .

This morning we have already heard wild shooting.

Towards evening, two small offshore boats were sunk in the port of Tobruk. Only small actions, we are hardly aware of them.

The Chief of Staff will contest Berlin's decision that the Afrika Korps receives no more decorations. We were told by the personnel office that we had received enough. In Berlin, they continue to imagine that we are conducting a war of leisure, as in the Balkans.

For the moment, it would be a mistake to believe that we will return home for good at Christmas.

. . .

3 June 1941

. . .

Pentecost is over. It seemed that the English wanted to make us forget this special holiday. Until this afternoon, their ships were firing particularly intensively at our positions, which maybe means that our air force feels relieved of their responsibility after taking Crete, as the English planes did not attack us. I wonder why we don't aim to take Gibraltar to open up free access to the Mediterranean for our submarines.

. . .

4 June 1941

. . .

Planes above us. Three Hurricanes were shot down yesterday. Otherwise, the day passed smoothly. Last night I went to see Rommel who did not feel well. He has a cold because he did not dry properly himself after his swimming in the sea.

All those comrades being transferred here now learn to know only the pleasant side of our existence here, not the difficulties and hardships that we have suffered while advancing through the desert.

6 June 1941

. . .

I would like to relive once again all our past years and the last two years this war. I firmly believe that we all will be back home at this time next year. Perhaps a ball will be organised for us in Gera? But a prolonged stay in the colonies cannot be excluded. Africa needs a colonial army. I have heard rumours in this direction that even officers should already have been selected. I would prefer to return to Germany. I am aware of having seen the worst part of Africa, but it is enough for me!

. . .

This morning, I got up at 4.30 hours to assist Rommel's departure for Sollum. I would have liked to accompany him, but I did not say anything to him because I think he would have asked me. But he has been always afraid that something would happen to me. The road between Tobruk and Bardia, our only supply road, is often the object of aircraft attacks at low altitude. The day before yesterday Gariboldi went by car to Sollum. Nothing happened to him, although he crossed a minefield to shorten his way. Shortly afterwards, ten English stopped one of our cars. A little later, they in turn were taken prisoner. They had taken a trawler on the southern coast of Crete and thought that the whole north coast of Africa to Tripoli was occupied by the British. Error!

Floods of letters to Rommel continue to arrive. Letters from people who have started collections for the members of the Afrika Korps, from girls who want to join us, as yesterday from a gym and dance teacher from

Bad Godesberg writing that she 'would like to be there and do something'.

Our supplies cause us a lot of trouble.

7 June 1941

. . .

We were nervous this morning as an English plane quietly circled above our heads, at an altitude of 2,300 m, out of reach of our flak shots. At that moment we picked up an uncoded radio broadcast, indicating among other things our precise position: 'Probably the headquarters of the Afrika Korps'. My first reaction was to tighten our security measures.

Yesterday afternoon, I learned that Walter had arrived at the staff. We met. We forgot for a moment that we were in Africa. He spent two hours with us. Of course, the official briefing by Wüstgefeld took up most of the time.

He saw Benghazi from above, a dirty hole, according to him, some palm trees, nothing else, and Derna, an Arab village. After four weeks in the desert he will say otherwise. Benghazi is for us the epitome of beauty and culture.

. . .

8 June 1941

. . .

Rommel returned sick from the front. This morning he worries me. Apart from awarding decorations to Italian officers, his schedule for the day is clear.

8 June 1941

. . .

I will not have the time to write to you tomorrow morning, as I leave with Rommel to Derna to attend a fantasia [an equestrian entertainment in the Mahgreb]. Departure at 7.00 hours. Some Arab tribes will demonstrate their equestrian art in his honour.

After I finished work with Rommel, he invited me into his car, 'the Mammoth'. I assured him that relations between his adjutants and the corps chief are as they should be. An atmosphere of cooperation and understanding has been established, essential for withstanding the long summer weeks.

. . .

I thank you a thousand times for writing to me constantly. You know that every one of your letters causes me great joy. It is the only joy I have outside the service, when we are forced to live so far away from each other.

My secretary passed by in the meantime. Yesterday I had criticised his work methods. I'm ready to admit that I'm not easy to work with, especially as the files have accumulated enormously. But it was not I who wanted this war!

. . .

9 June 1941

. . .

This morning, Rommel and I attended the event in Derna. Hundreds of German and Italian soldiers surrounded our car, directed dozens of cameras on the general, an interest which did not decrease during the celebration. Rommel had to struggle very hard to escape the undisciplined soldier-photographers. The event began. Suddenly, a Blenheim passed above us before disappearing. The Arabs and a large proportion of Italians ran away, the crowd became less dense, an agreeable consequence of this presence.

After the show, we went to visit General von Esebeck. He is in the air force hospital. He did not look at all well. I was shaken. It must be exhausting, first his injury, second every night English shelling, third the fact of being nailed to the bed in this climate. Afterwards we visited our own hospital. Rommel's coming caused a lot of joy to the soldiers with serious injuries and to the amputees. We had seen some shocking cases. Their confidence was encouraging. There was a very large number of cases of dysentery. After the tour, lunch at the Albergo, at the invitation of the air force, tables covered with white tablecloths and decorated with bouquets of flowers, armchairs: I enjoyed it!

That night, shortly before 5 a.m., I heard the engine noise of a plane. I feared an attack at low altitude. Two of our fighters hunted three English bombers and gunned down two near us.

. . .

10 June 1941

. . .

We need to be careful about what we are writing. Today, two letters of

Colonel von Herff were returned, opened by the department of counter-espionage in Munich. The author talked openly about everything and in terms similar to those that I use to write. He was lucky: the service in Munich has not sent his letters to Berlin first.

Our main transport route has become so bad that many cars break down. This and the growing number of our personnel staff created a major problem: the allocation of vehicles. Many of them did not work any more; others were repaired from spare parts of vehicles that had broken down. Other ones are always in the workshop.

The trucks available are no longer good enough.

Almost every officer has a big tent. Thanks to the English tents abandoned on airfields, numberless offices have been installed. The camp has lost its martial aspect.

We were told that in August the scourge of flies will become worse. Many people are already walking with a fly net over their heads. These and the large mosquito nets [in the tents] are very annoying.

. . .

12 June 1941

. . .

The Chief of Staff's stay in Berlin has been straining and exhausting because of the numerous interviews. He received fullest approval everywhere. Nevertheless he wasn't convinced that Berlin has a clear idea of the difficulties we face here. As for future policy, he did not want to speak to me at the moment. Still, I think that we'll come back to it during our 'informal discussions on the situation' in the evening. Rommel is thinking of leaving for Berlin in four weeks. Several events recommend it to avoid any misunderstandings that may prompt High Command to take drastic measures.

This morning, we were awakened around 6 a.m. to be told that a raft was floating on the sea This raft, now on the beach, was registered: 3rd Battalion of Sappers, Küstrin. Did the ship sink between Italy and Africa? The soldiers, did they drown? So in the water there is always a mystery that we can't solve. And the sea remains silent. Then not directly at our place, but 2,000 metres further on, corpses were washed ashore. Many sacrifices have been made to the Mediterranean.

For several days now, Rommel has been in a bad mood. One problem afflicts him very much. He believes that the merits of the Afrika Korps are underestimated. It really is necessary that he leaves for Berlin in four weeks. We hope that he will meet the Führer.

. . .

13 June 1941

. . .

You are wondering if you should take civilian clothes to Rome. But I am not yet sure that I will get leave. If I spoke about leave in my letters, made plans, it was the wish that was the father of my reflections. Even if High Command, in principle, agrees that I could go on leave and Rommel did his utmost to get his soldiers out of this dirt, we lack reliable means of transport to go to Italy and back. The Italians do not make it easy to transport supplies across the Mediterranean.

It is in a way a bit thoughtless to talk about it in a letter, as the day before yesterday we received five letters, returned by the postal service counter-espionage with complaints. Among them, there were two from a colonel stationed in Sollum. He will get a shock when he finds out that Rommel will take note of it.

. . .

Our Italian liaison officer no longer takes his meals at our mess: he installed his own mess. The tension does not reduce. Nothing is easy.

Yesterday, the president of the Italian Red Cross visited us, accompanied by a lady of a certain age, good looking. They distributed gifts: writing paper, socks, handkerchiefs, sweaters, chocolates and small Italian flags in silk for our entry (!) into Tobruk. Two women here in the desert! We hope that young ones will join us one day.

Rommel received countless letters again. It's amazing, what people say, 'Magnificent army chief'. This time there was a letter from a communist: 'Rommel, mass murderer, you deserve a bullet.' How awful that there are people like that in Germany!

Last Monday, our reporters left for Germany by plane. Owing to the lack of fuel, they had to make a forced landing near the Sicilian coast. They arrived on Sicily in an inflatable dinghy. All the film and letters were lost at sea.

. . .

14 June 1941

. . .

Starting tomorrow, I will make a copy of my letters to make sure they arrive.

A few moments ago, at 6 a.m., Rommel departed with the Chief of Staff to meet Gariboldi at Cyrene. He is on various matters very dissatisfied. According to our partners in the German-Italian Axis the Italians claim to have retaken Cyrenaica from the English. The Afrika Korps only assisted.

The fortress of Tobruk, still held by the English, troubles the overall situation and complicates the operations around Sollum. The English began to bombard us just now. The planes start at a low altitude while approaching and dropping their bombs.

. . .

I have been able to buy some cigars here. Don't worry. If there is nothing left to smoke, I just stop. Someone made a gift of 10,000 cigars to General Rommel for the units stationed in Sollum. Can they still be bought in Germany?

Members of the Afrika Korps will receive a band with the inscription 'Deutsches Afrikakorps', which was my idea. Then we will have new decorations, creating a medal between the Iron Cross, First Class, and the Knight's Cross. This measure will come too late. Soldiers have been decorated with the Knight's Cross who would have received the new insignia. It will be unfavourable to the war-wounded who can no longer fight. Why don't they accept my suggestion to give everyone of the soldiers who has distinguished himself some money to buy the decorations later they would like to wear? This would avoid a lot of anger and disappointment. We will be proud to wear the band which, hopefully, will become official one day.

15 June 1941

. . .

Yesterday, the English flew over us from morning until night. Gunfire all day. We have shot down four but unfortunately lost one. And today, it continues. Since 5 a.m., they bomb and attack us at low altitude. In addition, artillery fire. We do not know if the English have the intention to stage another attack before Tobruk. They attacked Walter across the front at Sollum. He will understand that the war here is very different, and much harder than the one raging on other theatres. Here, no village burns, no forests. There are no civilians fleeing. The war in the desert is worse than others.

. . .

While I kept Rommel company during his dinner yesterday, I made some suggestions on the situation. My impression is that I managed to convince him to consider the situation more seriously.

After Rommel had given his instructions yesterday evening, the cinema began with three documentaries, beginning with Hitler's anniversary. Music and odds and ends in the desert. Difficult to organise a better joke. The light of the screen could be seen miles away in the desert. English planes came up, end of the projection. Nothing occurred. One realised that there is something else in life apart from war, such as girls. It was, despite everything, a wonderful thing to see the films. Yesterday evening there was peace, this morning again war.

But our real enemies right now are the flies.

. . .

15 June 1941

. . .

The bombing began, as yesterday, at 5 a.m. Attacks at low altitude from the sea using the dunes. They have not yet discovered the gorge. This afternoon, they hit a bus parked in a nearby gorge, it burned. One dead. He was in his tent, writing a letter to his wife. This morning, they shot our petrol depot, leaving it burning.

The battle of Sollum, which I mentioned in my letter this morning, is not yet over . . . it will enter history as one of the biggest tank battles in this war, and especially here in Africa. Walter bravely resists despite English superiority. They came with a large number of tanks, including the famous Mark II tank. This tank is currently the heaviest and strongest in the world. We have shot about sixty and downed eleven Hurricanes. They have succeeded in pushing us off our positions, but they will return tomorrow from where they were coming. The question is, what will they do tomorrow.

. . .

17 June 1941

. . .

This is the third day of the battle of Sollum. Very harsh days for our soldiers. I hope that the losses will not be too high. The English attacked with considerable force, with an estimated 400 heavy combat tanks. We have encircled many of their troops. When you receive this letter, calm is likely to have returned to the front. Our soldiers are in need of rest after these days of combat which asked of them so much effort and extraordinary performance. Rommel had transferred all troops and the totality of the reserve to the front at Sollum. Once again, our partners, like us, a member of the Axis, the Italians, did not arrive in time at the front. 'Lack of gasoline,' they were saying. They generally cite a shortage of fuel or other technical failures when they are on the way to the front.

If the battle turns out well, which I expect, we will have witnessed one of Rommel's best performances. Why? Because he controlled his nerves and kept up. Moreover, he had the flair to wait for the impact of his actions despite the bleak news he was receiving – this at a distance of approximately 200 km.

. . .

17 June 1941

. . .

Although it is already 23.30 hours, I want to write a few lines quickly, because I don't think I can do it tomorrow, or even after tomorrow. I go with Rommel to Sollum to congratulate Walter on his great success. The battle is over. The English were not only repulsed with significant losses, but our troops were able to encircle a large part of theirs so that they had to surrender. We believe that we have captured between 180 and 200 heavy combat tanks. We do not yet have accurate information on the volume of the spoils, on our own losses or on those of the English. However, we already know that thirty-seven Hurricanes were downed during the past three days.

The past days had been extremely tough, at times literally very hot. Despite the triple superiority of the English, we won. This battle, which is essential for strategic and operational reasons, is a more remarkable achievement than the conquest of Cyrenaica. If we had failed here, we should have folded. We would have had to give up conquering Tobruk and many things more.

Obviously, we have been lucky, but as the saying goes, fortune favours only the competent. Rommel said that if he had been in the place of the English, he would have won the battle. This is not a sign of arrogance on his part, because the English were misdirected and had lost their self-control after they attacked the famous Halfaya Pass four times which has already been cited many times in newspapers (I make this remark for the person who eventually will open this letter), and finally abandoned the idea of a fifth attempt. Had they continued, our brave troops allegedly would have had to capitulate, as they were completely cut off since Sunday. And the Halfaya Pass is in a pivotal position for any advance. It is the most important tank battle fought so far. And we have won.

Therefore General Rommel was so delighted today that he has invited us to a glass of champagne. We emptied four bottles. It is too bad that at this moment our three reporters are not present to inform the German people about the performance of our soldiers and their success.

In the evening, we attended a beautiful spectacle. Next to us a Hurricane was shot down. The pilot, a Canadian, attempted to bale out with success, but the aircraft caught fire. Despite the low altitude, he managed to extricate himself from his plane and while running away fired wildly around with his pistol. Good for him!

. . .

22 June 1941

. . .

The plague of flies is worse than the heat. Hundreds swarm around us all.
Wednesday, the staff leaves for Bardia.

. . .

22 June 1941

. . .

Although Lieutenant Schultze-Brocksien feels sad to be leaving us, who remain together, he is delighted finally to return to Germany knowing that there is nothing that will hold us back here. We all would like to leave this dirty desert behind us to go there where life and movement are, a war as fresh and joyful as, from today, it is in Russia. I won a bottle of champagne from Behrendt who had said that, according to its own sources, we would never attack Russia.

119

This war was necessary, as the Führer maintains. I hope that it will end according to plan, scheduled, as it started. We might have another special announcement, as I do not think that the Russians will resist strongly. Wait and see. Hopefully this war will end in August to free forces for the eastern Mediterranean which would help us to advance. Will England be the next target? That would be wonderful. In that case, I believe that peace will come in early winter or that the war in Europe will be completely over in Europe, and will only continue in Africa against England and America. Then it is a question of who will still have the strength and the will to continue. So much for politics, which goes on, thank God, without us.

Today, Sunday, eight days since the English launched their offensive on Sollum. According to our estimates, they lost 1,000 men and 250 heavy tanks. Our losses are significant, but not nearly as high. After this defeat, will the English come back or definitively give up the fortress of Tobruk? These are the questions that concern us. I guess they could abandon their positions in North Africa and move their interest to Syria. But you always say, dearest, that I am never right. So wait and see.

On Wednesday, Rommel, General Gause and I drove through the desert, then to the east in the direction of Tobruk, back on the Via Balbia towards Bardia up to Capuzzo. The desert region is terrible. Rommel is full of thanks and wishes to keep Walter, the real winner of Sollum, as a commander. Then we went to congratulate the men who fought so bravely. Everywhere demonstrations of joy and shouting around the general visiting the front lines until nightfall. Next day, Rommel continued the journey to the famous, strategically important Halfaya Pass, where units have fought with bravery under the command of a captain of reserve, Bach, a pastor in civil life. He is likely to become the first clergyman to receive the Knight's Cross. He is an outstanding man who knows well to lead his soldiers.

. . .

We admired a landscape of great beauty, next to Sollum, the blue sea beneath. Part of Sollum is completely destroyed. Thus, I was for the first time in Egypt. We even visited Capuzzo, a desert fortress, completely destroyed and which, since we are in Africa, has changed the occupants five times. It explains the fact that there is not one stone on another.

23 June 1941

. . .

I might get leave from mid or late July. Under no circumstances before.

The current developments of the war in general, which might influence our situation in North Africa, are so exciting that, in all probability, the current pause will be probably short-lived. Starting today, we will have more news on the development of the operations in Russia. I hope that our assessment of the situation is correct, that we are not mistaken. What is the position of America?

If we have not yet moved into a World War, it now begins. It will expand into a clash between National Socialism and democracies on one hand, and other forms of government. This part of history will not be ended by a single victory on the battlefield.

. . .

24 June 1941

. . .

The Afrika Korps seems likely to be reorganised. It has in reality not been a corps for long: it is already an army. I am convinced that Rommel will get the command. Will I stay here at the staff of the Afrika Korps, or with Rommel? It will be decided in the coming weeks. Berlin has at this moment no time to spend for these questions and for us. First Russia must be conquered.

More unpleasant is the announcement yesterday that the field post has temporarily halted its shipments.

. . .

24 June 1941

. . .

Now, my beloved, this will be my last letter coming from the dunes. Tomorrow morning at 6 a.m., I accompany Rommel to Bardia. Much as I am glad to move 150 km further, I am reluctant to give up the beach.

Rommel speaks about going on leave. Today a lieutenant commander who had not seen him for weeks told him that he did not look well. It is true that he works too much and he does not like resting.

The reorganisation of the Afrika Korps will only be this autumn or after the victory over Russia. The war there has started well. This clearly shows again that the Führer had reason. England worked behind the scenes and Russia will stab us in the back one day.

Today, I received a letter from the father of Graf Baudissin. The letter that I had written on 15 April to inform them of the captivity of his son was not received until 1 June. The Red Cross had already informed him. His son had been transferred from Tobruk to Cairo, then to India via Palestine.

Yesterday, one of our guards captured three English very close to my tent. They had escaped from a prison camp at Derna and tried to reach Tobruk.

. . .

Bardia, 27 June 1941

. . .

Despite the clouds of flies, it was hard to leave the dunes and the wonderful location of my tent at this beautiful Mediterranean. The Chief of Staff objected to the move for several reasons: Bardia is near the front, Tobruk is in our rear with the Italians. Liaison with our squadron is not assured. The staff is divided into two groups, at a distance of 170 km. This decision places a strain on us and complicates the task. But we have overcome more serious problems. I have a feeling that the relations between Rommel and the Chief of Staff are deteriorating. One of the reasons is certainly their disagreement on moving. Very regrettable. Let us hope that I am wrong. But conflicts arise more easily here in the desert than elsewhere.

I just learned that two submarines 2 km from the coast have been identified. I gave the order for the anti-aircraft guns to shoot.

I am happy with our transfer to Bardia. I am assigned four large offices in a cool stone house with a beautiful view over the sea. This place is infinitely beautiful. If only there was no war! In the meantime, our guns fired, and very accurately. A periscope of a ship can be seen: we assume it is the topmost part of a vessel that has been sunk.

. . .

Bardia, 27 June 1941

. . .

Tonight, I went for a walk with Rommel and Lieutenant Colonel

Wüstefeld. We talked about the future location of the mess. We first thought of the mosque. To avoid a likely revolt of the Arabs, we then thought about the Catholic church, since it was half destroyed. But as Italians had laid flowers on the altar, I proposed to choose another place. Rommel agreed, which surprised me. It was decided that the Chief of Staff, followed by the rest of the staff, would join us here. He captured a second motorboat with four English on board. We do not yet know what their intentions, but we've got a motorboat now.

We begin again to wait for the English, who, according to recent news, are preparing something.

. . .

Bardia, 27 June 1941

. . .

Today, I had to formulate ten proposals for the award of the Knight's Cross. This is a huge job, since the motivation must be convincing. This requires a certain notion of strategy and a thorough knowledge of the circumstances.

We await very much successful announcements of the campaign against Russia. They should come soon.

. . .

Suddenly, at 12.45 hours, Rommel turned up in my office asking me if I wanted to accompany him. We visited up to 16.00 hours the former Italian defence installations inside the fortress. At their hasty retreat the Italian troops have dropped everything. Tents, bunkers and shelters, now more or less rotten, are still there as on the day they were abandoned: a huge quantity of ammunition, uniforms and other equipment, perhaps two to three thousand trucks, partly damaged or destroyed by the English looking for spare parts. An expensive Italian retreat, likely up to several billions. I should perhaps not to write about it. The censors have again returned some letters.

. . .

Bardia, 28 June 1941

. . .

Tomorrow, the Chief of Staff and his team will arrive at Bardia. Rommel will be less bored, as he will have more mail and can arrange more meetings. For him, resting means death, but he cannot always go to see the troops who have already to stand their own generals.

Rommel has received again at least a hundred letters today, plus parcels with lots of gifts. Among other things, some twenty pairs of shoes, some kinds of beach sandals. I am always amazed at what people are writing.

. . .

Bardia 29 June 1941

. . .

Six months passed and we are still in Africa. This is bad! But we should not grumble too much. Incidentally, the court martial has now sentenced to death a man who, in a letter to his father, vehemently criticised the war. Rommel must confirm the sentence, though I hope he won't. Who of us, gripped by the heat of the climate, the sirocco, artillery fire such as the members of the court martial have never seen, has not expressed his feelings on this kind of war which is not a war in a palm grove, in a letter, to feel better?

Today was the day of the special messages from Russia. Everything is very encouraging. It could mean that the war including a change of government and system will end at the latest in four weeks. What will happen afterwards? Advancing beyond Tbilisi, or to England? It would be nice if both could be done. Then there'll be the prospect that the war might be over this year.

Bardia, 30 June 1941

. . .

Walter confirmed the sentence, but said the soldier could present a plea for clemency. For Rommel and me, the sentence seems too harsh. This man, depressed at the end of a battle, wrote his father a letter, which was opened by the censors in Munich. The man had spilt his anger, but who of us has never done the same? We also have to understand the writer of the letter. He took part in an attack, exposed for hours to strong artillery fire, facing the enemy on the difficult front Sollum, standing the harshest climate and other conditions.

These are cruel effects. When the soldier finally had half an hour to himself, he picks out a piece of paper and confides to his father, whom he trusts. That the letter cannot be positive is understandable. The soldier probably could not fully control his nerves. I do not want to assist him, especially if he is a notorious criminal or a communist, as might be proved. In his war diary, he made reasonable comments. Rommel wishes to meet the judge of the court martial.

. . .

Bardia, 1 July 1941

. . .

The radio has just announced that Rommel has been appointed general of the Panzertruppe, a promotion that was surely decided by the Führer. Just two years ago, Rommel was still a colonel. A unique career.

. . .

Bardia, 2 July 1941

I am very doubtful of my chances for going on leave. The first group leaves this week and will return at the earliest in six weeks, and then it will be the turn of the next two per cent: one can calculate one's own dates for leave. Many believe that the war will end this year, to avoid another war winter for the people. We only can be convinced that everything possible will be done.

Today, the Wehrmacht Report announced the capture of 100,000 Russians. It's marvellous. I regret not being on the expedition. This campaign must be joyful and refreshing. Will we continue up to the Urals? We talk little about politics, but from time to time the question arises whether America is going to intervene in this war, and if so, how? These 100,000 Russian prisoners will be welcome to work in agriculture in Germany.

. . .

3 July 1941

. . .

Before Rommel went to bed, I got his signature for letters and documents that I had prepared for him. He retires at 2 a.m., totally exhausted. He has a huge amount of work to do from 6 a.m. I am observing it closely.

The Afrika Korps, alone on a big continent, has to do much more than any other corps. But it is not only Rommel: it is the same for each member of the Afrika Korps.

Today, it is particularly hot. At the same time, a violent sirocco is announced from which we don't suffer too much at the seaside. The English planes have been very active during the past two nights. Yesterday, they sank one of our 1,000-ton steamers carrying badly needed supplies. The previous day, another one was damaged.

. . .

Supply still poses many problems. In Germany, one does not understand the enormous difficulties facing us. Although our food is limited these days, there is enough. When it is hot, we do not eat a lot, but for our comrades who are building their positions at the front line, a can of sardines at noon and at night is not much. The hot meal in the evening is good, but varies little: noodles, dried vegetables, beans, sometimes peas. The dishes are well prepared. When during those days cigarettes and chocolate ran out, I complained. We, each of us, were finally entitled to twelve sweets. We can do without it, but it is nice to receive them from time to time.

. . .

Bardia, 4 July 1941

. . .

Our aircraft have been very active all day. Last night it was the turn of the English. They first made a loop over Bardia. As they did not see the slightest movement, they spun to the west.

Rommel plans to meet the Führer next week. We are already anxious for the information he will bring us. We spend our days with waiting, waiting and waiting! I begin to persuade myself that the English will not come any more, as no European can stand these high temperatures for action in the desert. It is truly admirable, the way our soldiers endure everything with such dedication.

. . .

Bardia 5 July 1941

. . .

This morning, I looked in the wadis along the coast, to find an appropriate location, if the English push us out of Bardia. Rommel recommended me to be careful, as yesterday evening a lieutenant was fired on nearby. I discovered nothing suspicious, but I stumbled again upon a huge stockpile of Italian artillery, tanks and batteries, abandoned during their hasty retreat, including ammunition and perhaps millions of shells.

It is actually a good sign that the field post delivered all your letters. But luck can change. The steamer sinking recently has unfortunately taken a lot of parcels to the bottom of the Mediterranean Sea.

. . .

Bardia, 7 July 1941

. . .

In recent days I have had more complaints than usual about food being not sufficiently varied. As we finished our reserves from the English booty, our soldiers have to eat the unbalanced German food: just noodles, beans, dried vegetables, sometimes sauerkraut, all prepared with poor-quality water and rarely seasoned.

Yesterday evening, I discussed matters affecting staff with Rommel. It became clear that the relationship with the Chief of Staff von dem Borne lacks warmth and cordiality. This is certainly one reason why nothing is really easy here.

All commanders want to go on leave, even those who have just arrived. A few moments ago, one of them came to see me. He looked so ill that he absolutely needed to return home. Most of them can't tolerate the climate and this kind of campaign. Our soldiers continue to suffer stomach pain. The personnel department in Berlin complains now of the high turnover of soldiers in the Afrika Korps.

Yesterday's air raid was harsh. But if Russia comes to an end, the air will be clear. After the campaign over there we could try to block the Mediterranean against the English.

. . .

Bardia, 8 July 1941

At the front: nothing new.

. . .

Despite full moon, the night was calm. We live like this day by day and are happy when we have no raids.

. . .

Bardia, 10 July 1941

. . .

Since the situation here is not yet clear, I am reluctant to go on leave. And I do not really want to take my days now. Leaving our beautiful Germany to return to this dirt here is too depressing.

Last night was calm, but an officer wearing Italian uniform has deserted to the English. He had inspected our positions and bases for several days. He introduced himself to us as belonging to a certain division, and another time as the officer of another Italian division. It could have been a genuine Italian officer (anti-fascist). I think rather that it was a cunning Englishman. He learned a lot. He came also to Bardia. Now, I suppose that we will soon be bombed. Only the English behave in this way.

. . .

Another example: a lieutenant went with some others to hunt gazelle. He observes a herd of camels. On one of them sits a man dressed as an Arab. A non-commissioned officer noticed that the Arab wears modern shoes. They approach and ask him to come down from his camel. He turns out to be lieutenant in the Royal Air Force whose plane was shot down five days ago. He was hoping to return by this means to the English lines.

On my desk, documents are piling up, many comings and goings, among them a lieutenant sentenced to six months in jail and demotion for having eaten his comrades' rations. He is certainly a bastard, but I think the sentence is too harsh. I don't support this man, but, once again, the court martial did not take into account certain essential circumstances.

. . .

Bardia, 11 July 1941

. . .

Tobruk is not likely to be the number one war objective for the moment. We are confronted by too many problems of supply. Tobruk, what an infernal hole! Rommel cannot position all his troops over there and not having anything here in case, against all odds, the English return.

Yesterday, a sensational event took place: six out of seven English planes were shot down over Tripoli. A joker pointed out that this success was due to an error of the Italians. In fact, in general the Royal Air Force can operate with impunity over ports as at sea. Even at sea they don't seem to be worried when they attack our cargo ships. A growing number of soldiers prefer to relinquish their leave rather than taking the risk of crossing the Mediterranean by boat.

. . .

Several of my father's letters, written between mid-July and the start of August 1941, disappeared in Germany after the war. My mother, like millions of compatriots left the Soviet Occupied Zone (East Germany) for the British Occupied Zone (West Germany) in 1947. She wanted to provide a decent future for her two children.

7

Clouds
5 August–4 October 1941

At the end of July 1941 my father accompanied Rommel to Berlin. Rommel met Hitler and Mussolini in Rome afterwards, and had talks with the Italian High Command. My father was able to spend four days in between with his family in the countryside in Pomerania. He saw the beginning of the harvest, inspected the vast fields of potatoes and wheat, and met neighbours. We had not seen him for several months. He was tanned, but emaciated and with sharpened features. He seemed to have changed somehow. Was it the war in general, the living conditions, the war in North Africa, or simply fatigue after his strenuous days in Berlin or was it the general situation in Germany and the lack of prospects for peace, which would have probably burdened him? I did not think about it very much, I was just glad that he had come to stay with us.

The days that my father spent with us were too short for him to recover and distance himself from the all-absorbing war in North Africa that awaited him on his return to Bardia. He felt sad when he left us and the familiar atmosphere at the countryside to join Rommel in Wiener Neustadt in Austria, to return with him to North Africa. My mother accompanied him to Munich where they separated.

My mother talked to me about this years later without going into details. She expected the visit of two former German officers, members of a military institute. They had been in contact with her because they knew that my father had belonged to Rommel's staff during the war against France in 1940, when Rommel commanded the famous the 7th Armoured Division. They knew that my father wrote regularly long letters to his wife. They knew probably also that Rommel had selected him from several candidates proposed by the personnel office in Berlin. They were interested in letters written during the campaign in France and those sent from North Africa. Those written in 1940 were lost in Pomerania at the end of the war, but my mother had managed to save those sent from Libya in 1941. The two officers looked for new information on the personality of Rommel, his strategy in North Africa, his relations with Berlin and with Hitler, his possible contacts with the resistance. They wanted above all to have a more accurate idea of my father's relationship with Rommel, about his influence on his personnel decisions.

After his departure and our return to Gera at the end of the holidays the daily correspondence of my parents reminded me of his absence every day. Letters arrived, sometimes several, then again days passed that the postman did not slide an envelope through the letterbox. Then I observed in my mother's face signs of unrest, signs which she tried to hide. She usually wrote her letters in the late afternoon. She avoided, as they told me later, showing in her letters her emerging concern about the war; friends advised her to be careful.

The fact that my father was fighting in North Africa did not interest me particularly at the time. I accepted it, because Germany was at war, without asking who had started it, how it could happen that, only twenty years after World War I, Germany was again at war. School and playing with friends in the garden and street were more important.

Our life in Gera passed without him. The town was famous for its theatre, which had once belonged to the Princes of Reuß, and its weaving mills. Its streets, old houses, the villa Kühn where we lived, surrounded by a magnificent park, reflected the rich relationship between the Princes of Reuß and the wealthy, active citizenship of the town. Villa Kühn was built by a family of industrialists in Gera who had lost the bulk of their fortune in the inflation raging Germany in the aftermath of World War I. The villa was the last remnant of their former wealth.

After the beginning of the offensive against the Soviet Union, I felt a change of atmosphere, first in Gera, but also in the Pomeranian countryside. My mother received the first notices informing her that comrades of her husband had been killed in action. Pages in newspapers began to be filled with notices marked with a cross in black, recalling the Iron Cross award. The absence of our fathers was, of course, a subject of discussion with my comrades at school. On the farms there was another picture. I noticed workers being called up for military service, to be replaced by a greater number of women during harvest time.

I associated a certain joyful excitement to the fragment of Liszt on the radio that announced military successes, not thinking about the environment of the event or the general war situation. The Department of Propaganda in Berlin had selected it. I took these announcements as a sign that indicated an early end of the war and the return of my father from the war front. From 1942 onwards they became rarer. I remember vaguely the hoarseness and exalted voice of Hitler promising victory and urging the German people to follow him to defeat the enemy.

My grandparents and my mother avoided expressing any comment on the war or on the internal situation in Germany in our presence. It was not always easy to hide one's irritation with this war, my mother told me after the war. Talking openly in the presence of strangers could be dangerous.

My parents' correspondence resumed.

Rome, 5 August 1941

. . .

I arrived in Wiener Neustadt at 12.45 hours. Everything was perfect. I had lunch in a hotel opposite the station, watery soup with three noodles, followed by potatoes and vegetables – very simple. And I hoped to have a good final meal! No sooner I had finished my lunch at the hotel that Rommel telephoned me at quarter past one to tell me that I absolutely had to go to have lunch with him and his family. Rommel, Mrs Rommel, Manfred, their son, and a nephew were already at table. Thus, I was entitled to a pair of sausages.

When I saw Rommel, I had a shock. He did not look at all well: he seemed to be completely down, his voice was weak and he had suffered quite a serious heart attack. I tried to persuade him to rest for a few days. But he believed his return was necessary. He was very pleased with his meeting with the Führer, though he gave me no details. I think that his poor health is due to a too rapid change of climate and possible severe anger during his trip. It is possible that people envy his solid position with Hitler and fear that he might play an even more important role one day.

He did quite well during the flight to Rome, but at the hotel he quickly went to bed. Tonight, dinner at the German residence, invitation of ambassador von Mackensen. Tomorrow morning meeting with Il Duce. Tomorrow afternoon, I go shopping. Mrs Rommel wishes to have a leather suitcase and a handbag. Even in . . . [Blacked out by the censor]

. . .

6 August 1941 (Rome)

. . .

Dinner at the Mackensens, served at 9 p.m. Apart from us and Mr and Mrs von Rintelen, there were two members of the embassy and Captain von Plehwe. The ambassador's residence is very elegant, furnished with antiques, surrounded by a park, well kept with a fountain and lit up. Moonlight covered the garden. The meal was excellent, very refined, for an embassy probably simple, the table decorated with taste and an attentive waiter for the guests. That is exactly what I like! The conversation was pleasant and easy going. It was pity that Rommel did not feel well.

This morning, Rintelen came to the hotel to accompany Rommel to meet the Italian supreme command. Afterwards he met Mussolini. He was not very happy about the outcome. He hoped for more support. The interview lasted one hour.

The Italians are not all very keen to keep the current front; they prefer to concentrate on Cyrenaica. Rommel, however, wishes to conquer Tobruk, which Hitler also considers necessary.

At 5 p.m., Rommel and I went to town to buy a suitcase. It was already too much for him: he was sweating and pale. It was high time that he returned to bed. With great effort, though, I was able to convince him to buy a handbag for his wife, who had asked me for it without his knowledge. He did not want to do it, absolutely not, and claimed never to have bought a handbag in his life. I quickly selected one and made him pay it.

It seems that the English are planning new attacks in Africa. More from Africa

. . .

Athens, 7 August 1941

. . .

We learned from the corps chief by telephone that Bardia suffered heavy air raids during recent nights. There are victims. The staff has been moving into a canyon. During day, work and heat, at night, raids. It complicates the situation.

I didn't think I'd write to you again in Europe. But on landing in Athens, Rommel's plane broke down. Repairs took all day. When his plane couldn't take off, Rommel fell ill again. He has a high fever. But he takes the view that, if he is not present in North Africa tomorrow, during the visit of the Italian Chief of Staff, Caballero, the Italians might decide to give everything up. Mussolini's decision will depend on the impression Caballero will get. Mussolini will meet the Führer in the next few days.

. . .

Back in Bardia, 8 August 1941

. . .

Coming back to Bardia after this trip, I felt rested, but I was shocked when I met the officers of the general staff again. Nobody looked well. They all need leave in Germany. The region is really too disagreeable; in addition during the last nights, with full moonlight, there have been bombings and raids at low altitude. The English – thanks to their espionage services – are well informed about us.

Everybody wanted to hear news from Germany. They all are longing to go home, even if they did not show it.

Since yesterday, Rommel has been intolerable. I had just withdrawn at about 00.30 hours when English planes spun over Bardia and nearby canyons, dropping parachute flares. Once one machine was gone, another arrived. Because they have not identified any target in the canyons or in the harbour, they bombed Bardia.

. . .

Bardia, 10 August 1941

. . .

Suddenly, in the morning, engine noise, and wild shooting: twenty-two English bombers and twelve fighters attacked the port. The anti-aircraft guns fired, but they all escaped. They are courageous.

If our planes do not come here soon, the English will retain control of the air.

Rommel and I were very fortunate during our return flight. Our plane crashed after taking off afterwards, three dead: the pilot, a lieutenant and a captain.

Lucky also was our squadron captain: his aircraft was riddled with bullets by two English fighters. At the very last minute, he managed to land his machine and jump. One of our patrols found him and took him back.

I had a lot of work to do today. I don't want anything else.

The international situation appears unchanged. Maybe the pressure that our troops exert on the Caucasus will play in our favour in Africa? For us, it is vital to feel the effects of it.

. . .

11 August 1941

My beloved, until now, comings and goings have been non-stop. Infernal! Twenty people at least showed up for interviews with me, long or short. All of them wanted to have a more or less lengthy consultation with me. Then the phone in between. I could not write a single line.

In a couple of days I will have been in Africa six months.

Our wish to spend Christmas in Cairo seems totally unrealistic.

. . .

Bardia, 12 August 1941

Today, Captain Lehmann, our doctor, advised me on the status of the health of the troops. It's upsetting. For this reason, Rommel has decided to move our reserve forces to the front by all costs. Given the high numbers of losses, it is high time to do it. I have fought for this decision, but we always lacked sufficient load room. The supply of food and ammunition will have to be second in priority.

A few minutes ago, I was just outside, in front of my door, for about half an hour. From the engine noise, you would have thought several planes were going to attack Bardia and surrounding areas. Although it was night and there was no moonlight, Bardia was bright as day. They dropped three bombs here, three there and finally on a low-flying attack, maybe just 100 m from us, another. It fell into the water, causing beautiful jets of spray. As it is an unusual bombing, on a night as dark as this one, I suspect they have learned something, either from their intelligence services or some treason. They surely knew that there was a submarine in the port. I fear we will have a tormented night, as also the situation inland is starting to become critical.

Hopefully, the war in Russia will soon be ended, so that finally the pressure on us will decrease. I am sorry that Baron von Neurath, son of the foreign minister and member of the same ministry, left today. He wanted to pass me a number of interesting ideas and reflections . . .

13 August 1941

. . .

Today I received all the letters from you that were missing. Tonight, I also received our two sons' letters. It reminded me of those four sunny days in Klein Silkow. Who knows when we will have such moments together again?

I intend now to be with you at Christmas. Time will pass quickly until then.

The situation in Africa has not changed, but I have a bad feeling.

. . .

14 August 1941

I am constantly concerned about our losses, caused either by war or by illness. Berlin does not grant us any reinforcements because of the numerous losses in Russia.

We feel that the British are slowing down preparations for their offensive. A spy or a traitor might have been active. Our enemies may have learned that the Panzergruppe Afrika has arrived. We always are trying to find out the reasons for their actions.

. . .

Restructured in September, the troops in North Africa were grouped into 'Panzergruppe Afrika' incorporating the Deutsches Afrika Korps (DAK), under the command of Lieutenant General Ludwig Crüwell, the 5th Light Division, the 15th Panzer Division under the command of my mother's cousin, General Neumann-Silkow, the 90th Light Africa Division and the 164th Light Africa Division. Rommel was entrusted the supreme command. My father remained adjutant (IIa) of DAK.

15 August 1941

. . .

Over our heads, another plane drops its bombs on the harbour and town. Isn't it strange? The arrival of a ship in the port was announced for today, but cancelled some days ago. It seems that the source of treason or espionage is not with us at Bardia, with the staff of the Afrika Korps, but somewhere else.

. . .

16 August 1941

. . .

Tomorrow is Sunday again. Two weeks ago, I was in Klein Silkow. In the evening, we went out hunting with our two sons with the beautiful scenery of our Pomerania around us, so far away from the war. Let's hope that a happy time will come again. The fact that some go on leave to Germany and others are returning is encouraging. It means that we can all go one day.

Yesterday evening, the Chief of Staff told Walter: 'Schraepler can go on the day he has a suitable successor and another IIc [deputy].'

. . .

I still prefer not to be moved for career reasons, as it will be too late to be appointed commander for the Russian campaign. But I think we should have the foresight to go on leave more often.

Lieutenant Wagner, a member of the staff highly appreciated for his energy and humour, returned from leave. On landing, his plane was attacked by two Hurricanes. He was seriously wounded by a bullet in the head.

In the meantime, Captain Behrendt and Lieutenant Colonel Wüstefeld arrived, the first with a bottle of real English whisky. We chatted for three hours and 'betrayed' Germany. Finally, it was midnight. Whisky is really a tiring drink!

Tonight, everything was calm until now, although a submarine has entered the harbour: his arrival was scheduled for yesterday, further evidence of treason or espionage.

. . .

17 August 1941

. . .

My beloved, can you suggest when I should take my leave? I could come in September or in October, which will exclude leave at Christmas. But I would like to be with you at Christmas.

. . .

19 August 1941

. . .

The day before yesterday, two English planes had made a forced landing; yesterday another. The pilots thought they were landing on territory occupied by English troops. They came from England, bypassing Malta.

The latest news from Russia was all very good.

. . .

20 August 1941

. . .

But, not all news is that pleasant. We have just learned that Lieutenant

Wagner died of his head injury. His death was deliverance for him, but his dynamism and sense of humour will greatly be missed.

. . .

Another story: an officer, who is suffering from an acute attack of dysentery and rheumatism, will be evacuated to Germany. He can no longer live in the tropics; thus continual comings and goings are happening in the Afrika Korps.

The night was calm, but we were severely bombed during daytime. We recorded 18 planes dropping 70 bombs.

. . .

22 August 1941

. . .

The funeral of Wagner was scheduled at Derna at 6 p.m. We drove for the first time on the ring road, 'Road of the Axis', leading around Tobruk. It was built by the Italians in eight weeks – 71 km! They are capable of doing it and do it with great enthusiasm. When we arrived, the coffin was already in the grave, a mass grave. The ceremony bothered me very much. Lieutenant Colonel Wüstefeld spoke some thoughtful words, followed by the pastor; his sermon was slightly confused. Salute. The grave hasn't even been filled in. The ceremony did not correspond very much to our military customs.

24 August 1941

. . .

Today, starting at 3.30 hours, planes bombed by releasing parachute flares. They lit Bardia and bays until about 5 a.m., in a wide radius around the port. Why? For the first time in this port, a relatively large ship, transporting fuel and spare parts, was expected at 4.00 hours. Somebody is betraying us. Another possibility: the English possess the Italian decoder. The ship continuously reported its times of departure and location throughout the day and that in the late evening the English Navy might attack it. After that we had no more messages. It was probably sunk. It is also possible that the British towed it into the port of Tobruk.

This is our war now: fighting against English air supremacy to protect our supplies.

No news from the front. Every night there are clashes between patrols, but nothing serious. In the meantime, reserve troops have finally arrived.

The day before yesterday, a large steamship sank near Tripoli. Almost all the soldiers were rescued. The cargo was lost.

Rommel wants to inspect the front near Sollum tomorrow. I wonder what he will bring in the way of information. He is often fairly optimistic.

We could meet in Rome early November, so you can do your Christmas shopping in Rome.

. . .

24 August 1941

. . .

Tonight, we spent two hours with Rommel. It is quite obvious that relations between him and the Chief of Staff von dem Borne are not warm. Rommel's ambition might be the cause. On the other hand, the Chief of Staff recognises his merits, guts, bravery and good intuition when it comes to assessing a situation. Myself, I am delighted to live this crucial time by his side.

25th August 1941

. . .

Tonight, we drank a few cocktails in honour of the departure of Lieutenant von Hößlin, who served before war in the 17th Cavalry Regiment. This farewell meeting started only at 22.00 hours after our day's work and after an air raid. We discussed the campaign in Poland, our experiences and the time when we were together in the Reichswehr.

Faced with this life in the desert, I do not like to think about our years in Stolp. It was such a beautiful time and is already so long ago, and you all are now so far away! It seems to me that all this was part of a previous life! Such years as we had in Stolp were unique, and will never return.

. . .

26 August 1941

. . .

I went to see the dentist today at 8 a.m. to check that my teeth are in good condition. Far from it. But he told me I do not have periodontitis. Our dentists are under the greatest strain because our teeth are suffering from vitamin deficiency caused by the kind of our rations we get.

My office will soon no longer exist. Of five employees, four have gone into the military hospital. Nine members of the staff caught hepatitis.

It is important that your father remains in good health so that he can manage his property during these years of war. After the victory, we will find a solution to ensure the future of this beautiful property.

. . .

27 August 1941

. . .

I wonder every day if it would not be better to spend my leave in Gera in October.

But why worry about the future now when the war is still on? First we have to win. We have a difficult winter ahead. Hopefully, we can finish the war in the spring. The next four weeks will be decisive for the Eastern front. If our troops don't achieve the capitulation of Russia now, future operations will suffer greatly from the deterioration of the climate and bad weather.

Tonight some shooting at sea. English artillery against our aircraft. So far, the English aircraft were quiet. They will probably come overnight.

A commander reported today that among the 1,100 men at his charge 948 were sick, suffering from stomach pain and intestinal infections. They continue to serve but are much less resistant.

I am fine again.

. . .

28 August 1941

. . .

The war has unfortunately become so merciless that one needs to learn how to deal with bad and sad news.

We are currently experiencing air raids at any time, day and night. Yesterday, the English discovered one of our ammunition depots and bombed it. And again today!

. . .

29 August 1941

. . .

I really wanted to go swimming, but again I had too many visitors today whom I couldn't ask to leave. Lieutenant van Nees stayed over an hour with me: he could not do without my tasty coffee, prepared by Pfistermeister. I appreciate it when they all come to see me, but they prevent me from working.

. . .

If we could meet in Rome at the end of October, that would be great! I do not like to establish a fixed programme prior to knowing the name of the new commander of the Afrika Korps, and the date of his arrival – also prior to the fall of Tobruk.

I have already started to look for a suitable successor. I found a lieutenant of a certain age. But he really wanted to go to the front. Now he has been stationed in one of our positions for three days, he has written that he would like to return. I can easily guess his reasons. They are obvious.

The situation has not changed. Planes repeatedly visit us, even just two hours ago. In the second half of the night, however, it was calm yesterday. Hopefully so today. But the moon is coming up, becoming fuller and longer. It promises us two unpleasant weeks.

. . .

30 August 1941

. . .

This morning they bombed a one of our fuel stores. At the moment there is exchange of gunfire at sea.

We received a special announcement today: according to it a special paragraph in the communiqué issued after the meeting between Hitler and Mussolini states that 'after the defeat of Bolshevism an era of peace will exist in Europe.'

The news coming in from London announces that Russia will lose the war. Has England finished with Russia? Up to know, it was said that the defeat of England meant the end of conflict. Now they say that the defeat of Bolshevism would end the conflict. Personally, I do not believe, despite all the optimists, that the war will end this year, nor next spring. The military operations in Russia can only resume late spring. Then the summer will pass.

. . .

Unfortunately, the number of illnesses is increasing. During these last ten days, more than 1,000 men were hospitalised. This is an enormously high percentage. Local experts say that intestinal problems will diminish by the end of August. By contrast, pneumonia will rise because it will be considerably cooler in the morning and in the evening.

I have not yet felt it, it is still terribly hot during the day. According to the Arabs, we were very lucky, because they had never known a summer so fresh. But this so-called 'freshness' is enough for me.

Before falling asleep at night, my thoughts are always with you.

. . .

31 August 1941

. . .

Maybe, the English also had Sunday. Their planes came only in the morning. On the other hand, no registered ship had been announced!

. . .

1 September 1941

. . .

At 19.15 hours the Chief of Staff and I were invited by colonel Crasemann for dinner. He had laid on a particularly agreeable mess. There, we could actually forget that we are living in the desert. For wallpaper, old Italian canvas painted with green oil paint. On the walls, a few pictures painted by a reserve lieutenant, old headlights for ceiling lighting and car seats for armchairs. In front of the mess some kind of porch, close to the cliff with a beautiful view of the sea and the moonrise tonight. The menu: melon as a starter, then broth with egg, roast gazelle, French fries and various salads, followed by canned fruit, accompanied by red wine. On the tables, white tablecloths, real cutlery and glasses. Everything was prepared with great care and kindness.

. . .

2 September 1941

. . .

The division has been hit very hard. High losses.

. . .

4 September 1941

. . .

The day before yesterday, after midnight, I had just finished writing a letter to you, when, as so often, I heard one or two planes flying over Bardia. When a bomb exploded next to my house, I hoped that it would stop. But the same aircraft returned. After describing a semi-circle, it dropped a big bomb and three smaller ones directly on my house. The big one hit the right corner, the two smaller ones the wall on the right side and a third the entry to the air-raid shelter. The explosion of the first bomb was already considerable and the blast enormous, but the next four bombs were outrageous.

Window frames, doors flew out of their frames, walls stripped of their plaster. Debris everywhere. I found myself in a cloud of dust, which you might expect to experience once, but not twice. It was awful! Worst of all was the howling and singing of the approaching bombs and this strange and alarming feeling that they are coming straight for you. The seconds lasted an eternity. Out of the house! Impossible, because I was caught up in my mosquito net. Lt Col. Wüstefeld and I were examining the damage when more planes approached and we were targeted again. From now on I shall go into the shelter. One won't be lucky twice.

. . .

4 September 1941 (evening)

. . .

If the English, who surprisingly did not come last night, have come back with so much fire power we'll go to sleep in the desert to avoid bombs falling on our heads. I put my camp bed in my car and I am off to sleep in the desert! We are in a twilight zone, deciding whether we should leave Bardia for the night or not. The mess yesterday was enough; we do not want to have it again.

Today, the planes have already dropped some bombs, not counting their attacks at low altitude on the front line.

The Chief of Staff, making a great effort to keep me in my present position, informed me that Rommel and General Gause had agreed to retain me in my current position, since I am indispensable. The risk of being transferred to the Panzergruppe is thus avoided.

. . .

5 September 1941

. . .

We should not make plans in wartime. Yet, we tend to do so, even if we are annoyed when things go differently. When we are at war, we have to live from day to day, nothing else. Regarding Africa, Berlin's position, which is all to familiar, irritates us: 'Nothing is really happening in Africa.'

I'll go only hunting gazelle when we have a chance of coming upon some. A trip through the desert without shrubs and trees, just dirt, only stones and camel thorn, is stupid and without poetry. Do you know that in Italy they are dancing a new dance? 'One step forward, two steps back, once around the axis and cling to your partner.' This is the so-called monkey dance. If the censors open this letter, they will have something to ponder on. But enough for now.

. . .

6 September 1941

My beloved, I spent a terrible day. I wanted to clear the files piled on my desk, but I wasn't successful. A crowd of visitors came, one after the other. I can't list them all, so many came. If everyone gave me a silver coin, I would be a millionaire.

During the night, we experienced two successive bombings, separated by a brief interval. I learned this morning that it was one of our own, obliged to make a forced landing. It spent its bombs to avoid the worst. The pilot could have dumped them into the sea! I got up at the first engine noise. And it was a German plane!

I lost at cards so badly so that the Chief of Staff said, 'You must have a wife who is very much in love with you tonight'. Is this true?

. . .

7 September 1941

. . .

According to the latest news, Christoph von Platen was appointed commander of a reconnaissance unit in Russia. His wish was finally fulfilled! I hope he can stand it. Russia is costing us a lot of our forces and requires great commitment on the part of everyone. If only things over there don't come to a halt. It won't be any easier in spring. And us here in Africa? Do we remain on stand-by? The weather conditions make the general situation in Russia worrying.

. . .

10 September 1941

. . .

Today, my captain did not feel well. I hope that he doesn't become ill. He is a tall, strong man who has already lost at least 15 pounds. I don't understand why. Here we have a blue sky, sunshine as in Germany, a climate as cool as at the Baltic Sea, and yet disease is rampant.

I have a new idea for my leave. You come to meet me in Rome on 15 December, next day we go together to Gera. I could stay until 2 or 3 January. Isn't that a good idea? But maybe you need these days to prepare for Christmas.

. . .

11 September 1941

. . .

The Chief of Staff is transferred. His successor will be Colonel Bayerlein. My turn will be next.

There is no need to bring my civilian clothes to Rome. You can walk around in uniform. It's different in the south, unlike Germany.

. . .

12 September 1941

My beloved, for the first time in eight days, I went out for a swim. But I came back: it's already too fresh to stay on the beach.

The Chief of Staff believes that Rommel wished to replace him. He probably wants to build up a new team for the continuation of the war.

Currently, there are no signs that the English prepare a new attack.

Last night, we did not have English planes visiting again. The Italian air defence shot down several planes, among them the one which had regularly bombarded us.

Yesterday, we observed three English submarines.

. . .

My English car has problems. It is difficult to obtain spare parts. The shells around us in the area are completely emptied. It is imperative to organise new spare parts.

Captain Schultze-Brocksien, now in Germany, writes that his only nephew was killed in action.

. . .

14 September 1941

. . .

I still have some time to describe you our tour into Egypt this Sunday. Why not spend a Sunday over there? In peacetime, a visit would be more pleasant than today, with the bombs and grenades.

This morning, we left at 4.15 a.m. to join a unit we wanted to accompany. On the way, we met Rommel and talked with him. He wanted personally to direct the surprise of the English in their camp. Alas, they were informed. They had gone before we got there. Three prisoners.

But the Panzergruppe seized a truck containing the office of the regiment. The records and mission orders found there might be valuable. Of the alleged camp no trace, an empty nest. Our advance has progressed as planned and we stay hard on their heels. For many reasons as you can imagine, Berlin has forbidden Rommel to undertake further actions, especially since some vessels have disappeared, either sunk or seized by the English. I am afraid that the English interpret this decision as a weakness on our part. The English greeted us during the operation several times with bombs. Two vehicles carrying petrol were hit by a bomb. They were completely burned out. Huge clouds of black smoke. Four dead and six wounded. Today, there is nowhere to hide from reconnaissance aircraft, especially in the desert.

German and Italian aircraft were very active. But eleven Italian aircraft are missing; only the squadron leader came back. He followed a group of German Stukas. It is believed that the eleven planes were forced to land because they were short of fuel and were not shot at by the English. I do not believe in this version of events because the Italian aircraft that collaborate with us have always been outstanding.

Yesterday, a small operation on Tobruk was successful. If censors read this letter, it will certainly be returned. But really it contains nothing that is untrue or might reveal future intentions.

. . .

15 September 1941

. . .

146

They speak about me as a child prodigy who gets shown everywhere because of his 'good' appearance and his solid constitution. I hear it at least once a day, regularly from Rommel. That is why I do not understand why our comrades fall constantly ill.

I just received information about our losses yesterday. I am appalled. The English air raids were of great effect. Up to our departure, I only witnessed three bomb attacks, but then there was further bombing. We lost tanks and vehicles. However, the actual venture has not caused a single loss. On then return, a company of panzers has disappeared, probably lost its way. It is possible that the English have got them. As much as I was enthusiastic about yesterday's operation, I see it in a different light today. The English will be certainly delighted. Our only loot is the office, the contents of which will be interesting. But one thing remains unclear: why did they take it along with them into the desert?

We have just had an exciting evening. An armoured company was sent to search out tanks left in the lurch. We feared that the company was surprised and captured by the English. After our operations, the English proceeded and counter-attacked on the right and left.

Our planes warned the commander of the company that his situation wasn't very good. But for some unknown reason, he continued to advance on to his mission. Hence, discussions, measures, instructions, and finally information from the Panzergruppe, which in turn had informed Rommel. Then new instructions, which were considered inappropriate by the Chief of Staff of the Afrika Korps. Meanwhile, it was midnight. While these events occurred, English planes bombed the port, having learned about the arrival of a submarine, but the arrival of the submarine had been cancelled. Once more, treason. And finally a shot. When we looked toward the port, one of its headlights covered the water. A coast guard was hurled by the pressure-blast into the water from his post high up. He was not found. As telephone communications didn't fail, we finished playing cards.

. . .

16 September 1941

. . .

Losses of officers are extremely high. The state of health of the troops is deteriorating more and more. Where will it lead to? According to you, I am too optimistic, but I begin to be pessimistic about the situation. Ships continue to be sunk, and the overall situation does not improve.

The recent operation was nevertheless a big setback. Command is held responsible because he should have acted differently. But after the event, you're always wiser and can always see how you could have avoided losses. The armoured company that caused us a lot of trouble has come through, back to its division with skill and without any losses.

. . .

17 September 1941

. . .

Three excellent officers were killed in battle, among them Colonel von Unger, commander of the 6th Schützen Regiment [formerly 14th cavalry regiment]. I had a high esteem for him. When looking at the number of losses I am worried. On the other hand we seem to advance quite well. I hope that the troop will withstand everything.

Lieutenant Colonel Wüstefeld has told everyone, go to Schraepler if you need something good. You will get new cars, an excellent aide and delicious pancakes as well.

The English have dumped their bombs on us today. Why not do it again during the day? Otherwise, I can't complain.

. . .

18 September 1941

. . .

Heavy storm from the north-west, wind-force eight. It sends dust into every corner. Despite the weather, a plane has dropped four large bombs at low altitude – because of the storm and darkness in the port. Today at noon, twenty English planes have made us happy, followed by six others. They really seem to want to disturb our peace. An English patrol appeared at the Halfaya Pass. It was repelled . . .

Bardia, 19 September 1941

. . .

It is said that during the night yesterday the English had suffered very heavy losses. They left two dead, a lieutenant and a corporal: this was out of character for them when it comes to smaller operations.

The day before yesterday I received a letter from Commander Appel, who feels better; he invited me after the war to hunt a pair of capercaillies. . . .

20 September 1941

. . .

General Müller-Gebhard took yesterday's letter. He left here last night to catch a courier plane taking off at 6:30 at Derna. This morning I heard his car had been found, wheels in the air, at the foot of a steep slope. But it seems that nothing had happened to him. I was worried letting him go in darkest night. But I was thinking more about English patrols than hills.

You write again about the coming winter and that you are worried about having sufficient coal. These problems will not stop for the time being. We, on the contrary, we are still in shorts, and regularly grumble about the cold wind. But at noon, it is still as warm as summer time in Germany.

I am worrying about some of my letters. It is not pleasant to see letters sent back by High Command with charges of 'defeatism' [a second-rank accusation from the censors], and then [worrying about] being summoned before a court martial. At the moment letters are constantly sent back by the censors, who are objecting in part to petty little matters and ridiculous remarks more than information. It seems that the censors are particularly focused on African events.

Schraepler is always fine. He looks so 'healthy'. This is how they present me everywhere, as a miracle, because it is unofficially claimed that Europeans can't last here more than six months. 'Unfortunately,' is my usual reply.

I am still thinking that you could pick me up in Rome and that we could go to Germany together. Germany is so beautiful that one cannot describe it, as one officer put it the other day.

I don't think that I shall get to Cairo, at least not during this campaign.

. . .

21 September 1941

. . .

The farewell to the Afrika Korps was hard for the Chief of Staff. When we shook hands at length, there were tears in the eyes.

Meanwhile, I met with my new sergeant. He made an excellent

impression on me, eleven years in the army, trained by the Reichswehr and he belonged to the 12th Cavalry Regiment. I only fear that he wants to go to the front to become an officer.

News from Russia is good. The war there might be finished within four weeks.

. . .

22 September 1941

. . .

Two sympathetic lieutenants just visited me, transferred here on my request; one will be the personal aide to the future general commanding the Afrika Korps, Crüwell, the other will have same function for the new Chief of Staff of the Afrika Korps, Colonel Bayerlein. I found likewise a very good aide for Rommel.

This morning, I left for Capuzzo for a couple of hours. I visited the area selected for a cemetery for our comrades who were killed in action. One day it will be very beautiful.

. . .

23 September 1941

. . .

Today, a special announcement about military successes in Russia. Hopefully we will have more of them. The army accomplishes great things there. If favourable weather continues, further successes can be hoped for. Should I be transferred from here, I would like to be appointed either battalion commander or at a staff.

. . .

Bardia, 24 September 1941

. . .

At noon, the English dropped sixty bombs on our munitions depot. Nine planes were shot at Sollum, five by one lieutenant alone.

We just had experienced a night-time bombing. Bardia was lit up as in broad daylight. They accurately launched two firebombs at the military hospital. Part of the building started burning. About five deaths and as many seriously injured. The English knew full well that this building was a hospital. It was theirs before they retired. In addition, with all the light in the city, they could see the Red Cross sign on the roof. We had no water, so the building hit by bombs burned down completely.

. . .

26 September 1941

. . .

When you read these lines, eight weeks will have passed since we saw each other last. It was wonderful that everything worked so well. Who would have thought looking at how things turned out that I would have got permission for leave then!

Some seriously injured men died at the main first-aid post. The bombing of the military hospital has cost us eight deaths.

My beloved, it is possible that you will arrive in Rome before me. We could meet at the Hotel Excelsior, if I am not at the station. This is the best hotel, and for us it will be just fine. Tonight, we had another special announcement, that 544,000 prisoners in Russia have been captured.

. . .

27 September 1941

. . .

During the day, everything was upside down. You can imagine how many bombs will be falling tonight, if they come back! Until now, they have failed to hit our cockchafer [code word for a transport ship].

And again it rained bombs. Unfortunately they killed a lieutenant, with whom I had had a long and interesting discussion. I feel particularly sorry. The blast from those bombs catapulted Pfistermeister, who was slightly injured. But he was able to resume his work immediately after a visit to the doctor. I saw two burning aircraft plunge into the sea. Six aircraft are supposed to have been shot down.

. . .

28 September 1941

My beloved,

I really needed a real Sunday nap, but the infernal engine- noise of the aircraft prevented me. In addition, the post warned us every twenty minutes of the arrival of aircraft, i.e., we should go into the shelter.

Our fighters are active from the very early morning until late at night.

Nevertheless, the English reach their goal and bomb, especially if our fighters fly too high. Our cockchafer is still swimming, but last night some of the fuel already unloaded was hit by bombs. A huge impressive torch.

. . .

Yesterday morning, a dozen bombers attacked the munitions depot. Powerful detonations. An English reconnaissance aircraft approached, which probably wanted to see the outcome. He had observed a lot of activity in the harbour. Then it really started. Unfortunately not all the bombs disappeared in the water, but they increased the number of craters in Bardia. Some men, sad to say, died. Wüstefeld was lucky. He was just on the way to the bunker, heard whistling and threw himself down. It killed a lieutenant and a corporal who were about to take refuge in the shelter. He was a lieutenant of quality, particularly sympathetic, with whom I had a few moments earlier a long conversation about telecommunications. Intense firing by our air defence followed.

The searchlights have done a good job. The shots were accurate. It was fascinating to observe the manoeuvres of the aircraft trying to escape the spotlight: loopings, rollings and so on. They returned to bombard us at 4.30 and 5.30 hours. All together seven aircraft were shot down. This festival will surely continue and I fear that submarines are lurking near our freighter in the Mediterranean. It is a very hard life for the German crew.

As far as health is concerned, it is especially difficult. The climate does not heal the wounds. Some ulcers appear because drought, heat and dust form scabs, but under the scabs are abscesses, pus. Minor injuries, such as scratches, degenerate into infections that won't heal.

. . .

29 September 1941

My darling and beloved,

I would like to be with you so much today, for our tenth wedding anniversary, and to be alone with you after dinner to recall the past ten years that have been so beautiful, and make sure that the next ten years will also be beautiful, and even more beautiful to offset our current separation.

A few days ago, I hoped to be sent on a mission to Berlin. But our colleagues there are only happy when they receive no one who comes from the front and causes extra work. So the more eagerly do I prepare my leave early December to find you in Rome. In ten weeks! In Rome we shall make up for missing the anniversary of our wedding day.

No sooner had I climbed into my car last night, to get shelter at night, than the bombing festival began. Ninety minutes. But it was less dramatic than the day before yesterday. The planes flew high to avoid the floodlight. They dropped eighty-two bombs. Our cockchafer was not hit. The damage was not too great. This time, they applied a different strategy, arriving individually but in permanent detachment. One dropped his bomb, left, and another came, each time from a different direction.

. . .

30 September 1941

. . .

Today, I had to tell two soldiers of high quality, sons of farmers from the Mark Brandenburg and Silesia, that they could not go home to dig. The war situation would not allow it.

I heard the following story: during a recent bomb attack, the car of the Flak commander was badly damaged by one bomb, and a second swirled through the air. When his adjutant began to recover his things, at least what was left, he found among the remnants of the car an impressive snake 1 metre long, a most poisonous one! He was lucky that his car was hit by a bomb and broken into a thousand pieces.

. . .

We shouldn't think yet about having a party in our own four walls one day. I can't believe that peace is a long way off. We'll probably not have it this year, certainly next year. October next year, we shall be together again.

Your mother mentioned in her letter that two sons of von Mannteuffel and the second son of another neighbour in Pomerania were killed in action. This news shakes me very much. This war causes us more grief than World War I, because it spans a relatively short period. I find it difficult to imagine how, after the war, the officers' corps will be able to recover. Young men will be missing for years. It will pose a great problem.

. . .

1 October 1941

. . .

Today I am really angry with Rommel. According to instructions from

Berlin, we have the right to send 2 per cent of the troops on leave, which is not much. But when Rommel came today, he said there were too many soldiers on leave! He then learned that these figures do not include soldiers declared unfit by the medical officer who have to return to Germany for treatment. For Rommel, this was too many. He demanded that a total of only 2 per cent leave. Accordingly, this means that those being in good health won't go as the number of patients and those in need of treatment is too great. Rommel once took a different view.

An English plane flew over us for more than two hours. Do they know about a ship about to enter the port that we don't know about yet?

At the start of November, I can maybe tell you with some certainty whether I can come at Christmas. I really would like to stroll with you in Rome for two days!

A month has passed again. It's terrible, how time passes quickly.

For three days, there is good news, but nothing specific, about the situation in Russia.

. . .

2 October 1941

. . .

Wüstefeld has conferred the Iron Cross on deserving members of the engineering battalion who have distinguished themselves during the bombing. They were so full of emotion that they were closer to tears than smiles. Apart from the battalion of pioneers, they generally had little chance of being decorated with the Iron Cross.

This morning, Colonel Dießner visited me. This gentleman, 60 years old, is our liaison officer with the Italian troops. He has just lost his son in Russia.

I received a letter from my driver's father asking for permission for his son to leave the army because his other son was killed in action. He needs him for his business. I was forced to reject his request. When I expected his return at the end of his leave I found out that he had been taken to a military hospital in Germany. It happens to many soldiers, that they fall ill at home when on leave, and are eventually declared sick.

I haven't yet told you that the English have systematically bombed German military hospitals. Our military hospital in Bardia first and, on the following Saturday two more on the road to Tobruk. More than twenty dead and a large number seriously injured. We wanted to take appropriate counter-measures.

. . .

3 October 1941

. . .

The new Chief of Staff, Colonel Bayerlein, arrived here yesterday evening at 23.30 hours. We talked together until 00:30 hours. At noon, we had another conversation for an hour, and again tonight. I am impressed by him. He does not waste time on trivial matters and he knows what he wants. An optimist. His information brought from Russia is interesting and he report on situations that we did not know about. I believe that our cooperation will be very positive. The media have a good opinion of him.

He told me that Keitel was certain that I was leaving for the Panzergruppe with Rommel. Keitel thus looked, with Crüwell, for a qualified adjutant for Crüwell, but had not found one. He [Crüwell] was glad to learn that I was staying with the Afrika Korps. Bayerlein told me he [too] was happy to hear that I was still here.

Last night, we suffered a plane at low altitude firing wildly with his machine gun. There is always something on.

4 October 1941

My beloved,

You spoiled me, sending me so many letters! For the letters I received yesterday, I thanked you already last night rather late.

Wim gave me another one today, and when I returned from the mess around 20:00, I found two more and a small package. Now, I have all your letters up to No. 51 of 27 September. You cannot imagine the effect if one receives so many letters in the dirty desert on a Saturday night! It's wonderful. For an hour and a half I have been reading them. I think this is a record.

. . .

At the moment, I am glad not to be transferred, especially as I know what it'll be like in the East in three weeks' time, at the beginning of winter.

. . .

Momentum and vitality is what we are lacking now. Willingness and readiness depend on so many different conditions.

Our ship, the cockchafer, which brought us a rain of bombs and which we watched leaving, full of apprehension, has arrived all right in Italy. The boat and its crew have been lucky, perhaps because, in recent days, the Italians have continued to be trounced by the English fleet.

My beloved, you don't really want to come to Rome in December. Time before Christmas is too short, while you will have more time after Christmas and you will be more relaxed after. I understand this perfectly.

8

General Erwin Rommel

In his letters of 1941, my father did not indicate any possible links between Rommel and the German resistance. Yet, when reading his letters, especially those written in September, three months after the entry into war against the Soviet Union, I found that my father noted a certain reserve on Rommel's part towards him in their daily contacts.

As Rommel was appointed supreme commander of the Panzergruppe Afrika in August, his impression seemed to be confirmed. Rommel did not assign my father adjutant of the Panzergruppe Afrika general staff, and he remained adjutant of the Afrika Korps, commanded by General Ludwig Crüwell, Rommel's successor in this post.

Nevertheless, as I read the letters, I could see my father's position change later, taking Rommel's generally cautious attitude as the explanation. (My father suggested it vaguely in his letter of 22 October 1941, picking up for my mother a discussion which he had with General Crüwell.) This rather sudden change in Rommel's attitude towards my father became perceptible around August and September 1941; perhaps it can be explained by Rommel's wish not to involve anyone in a problem area that concerned him alone – my father knew him too well and might have guessed his state of mind. Rommel, an ambitious and competent officer, educated and trained in Prussian military traditions and values, might have been looking with critical eyes at the changing political situation and the effects of this war which had started out and spread from the ambitions of National Socialism and his Führer, his commander-in-chief. Rommel might have sensed the danger of these reflections for him, his family and others, realising that in his position he could not speak to anyone about them. Prussian military values, having influenced the development of the members of the Reichswehr that became the Wehrmacht in 1935, had nothing in common with the amoral behaviour of Hitler and his followers: but there was a deep contradiction that might explain the malaise, crystallising in certain members of the Wehrmacht, that finally engendered a feeling of uneasiness about Germany after 1933 and about the evolution of the war, even if some high-ranking generals were motivated by personal ambition to turn to Hitler's line.

After Hitler seized power on 30 January 1933, several assassination attempts were attempted, which were unsuccessful for different reasons: technical failures, changes in Hitler's programme at the last minute, or some other problem.

Initially, the communists were the largest group in the resistance movement. They stopped opposing the regime on the orders of Stalin after the signature of the Soviet-German Non-Aggression Pact (1939) but resumed it at the beginning of the Russian campaign. The non-communist groups included all sorts of people: socialists, officers, civil servants, trade unionists, representatives of the church and others.

But as long as Hitler's foreign policy achieved success, any opposition, any resistance, any criticism, any move of opposition could be viewed by the population as an act of treason. Acts of opposition or resistance would only get public support if the situation on the front and inside Germany worsened noticeably in any way. Only then would peace at any price be preferable to the futile pursuit of war.

The resistance, led by the military, considered the time after the Casablanca conference (January 1943, when Roosevelt announced the intention of the Allies to force Germany to an 'unconditional surrender') and the defeat at Stalingrad (February 1943) was appropriate for action.

On 20 July 1944, Colonel von Stauffenberg tried to assassinate Hitler in his headquarters in East Prussia using a bomb hidden in his briefcase. The Führer escaped the attack, slightly injured. After this episode, the Gestapo and the SS launched a wave of terror and repression against members of the resistance, their families and friends. They executed them in dishonourable ways and murdered thousands of them in the camps: every type of person that had in any way associated with the resistance movement.

After the unsuccessful 20 July plot against Hitler, a widespread investigation was conducted to identify possible participants. Rommel was identified in some documents as an acceptable military leader who could be placed in a position of responsibility should the coup succeed. No evidence was found to link Rommel directly to the plot. Rommel ended his life in October 1944, forced by the regime to commit suicide.

The change of attitude toward my father, beginning a few weeks after the attack on the Soviet Union (22 June 1941) that reduced the prospects for success of the Afrika Korps/Panzergruppe Afrika, might indicate Rommel's intention of keeping his feelings on the expanding war and his dilemma to himself.

For Rommel observed that my father within his job regularly received all kinds of visitors, from the front, from Berlin, from all over. He certainly knew that my father's tent was often filled with visitors until late at night and that they discussed the service, the war, the front, life in Germany, their families and the time they spent with their regiments before the war. Naturally the subject would turn to his strategic intentions or simply exchanging ideas on everything and anything linked to their life in Africa, while having a coffee or a drink, prepared by my father's aide. And Rommel could assume that my father knew what he was saying or writing, and that his letters might receive the special attention of certain people in Berlin.

Faced with the overall development of the conflict, as the situation threatened to escalate with the entry into war against the Soviet Union, a man in Rommel's position – both envied and criticised by some members of the High Command – had above all to avoid everything that could reveal his thoughts (doubts?) about the course of the war to the Führer and those near him. Given the dangers that he and his family would risk, Rommel probably decided to change his entourage as soon as an opportunity was given to him. It came with the restructuring of the German troops fighting in Africa, the creation of the Panzergruppe Afrika, at the head of which he had been appointed.

Another motive could have been that Rommel wished to leave a competent officer at the side of his successor at the Afrika Korps, General Ludwig Crüwell, who was close to the new leadership of the Panzergruppe Afrika, someone who had lived in North Africa since the start of the war front there, someone reliable in whom he could place his confidence. Rommel's decision was a sign of his strategic aim of fulfilling his mission in North Africa and it showed at the same time his continued appreciation of my father. My father's letters to my mother support this interpretation, in spite of occasional critical remarks on certain decisions made by Rommel; and this has also been confirmed by one of my recent discussions with the former Mayor of Stuttgart, Manfred Rommel, son of the general, who sent me his father's reflections.

The war against the Soviet Union, the main objective of Berlin, could not be terminated before winter 1941. In Africa, Rommel's advance had been condemned by the British counter-offensive, Operation Crusader (November 1941–January 1942), by the lack of reinforcements and supplies, one of the consequences of the exhausting front against the Soviet Union, by the practical absence of the Luftwaffe and by the limited industrial capacity of Germany, which could not furnish sufficient supplies to two hard-fighting fronts, especially when the Russian front occupied first place on Hitler's list of priorities. This is certainly one reason why the shortages began to be felt seriously in Panzergruppe Afrika, particularly during the last quarter of 1941 and the beginning of 1942, in the face of well-equipped British troops. Another reason according to my father's letters was the heavy bombing of German positions and of the cargos coming across the Mediterranean with supplies, and the concomitant side-effect of demoralising the combatants in Africa. Rommel was forced to abandon the siege of Tobruk during this difficult period and to retreat while suffering important losses, attempting later, 1942, to regain lost ground.

Rommel was forced to abandon the siege of Tobruk during this difficult period and to retreat while suffering important losses, attempting later, in 1942, to regain lost ground. The strategic ambition of the Italo-German axis had been to damage vital British interests by the occupation of Egypt, the Suez Canal and the Red Sea region, the latter providing the shortest access to the Indian Ocean, the British colonies and offering direct contacts with the Japanese fleet in the Pacific. And Rommel advanced his panzers practically to the gates of Alexandria, just a few hundred kilometres from the Suez Canal, almost chasing the British forces out of the region. But the situation changed some time after the aggression of the Soviet Union in June 1941. Faced with the British supremacy, Rommel was forced to retreat, yet he did not lose his prestige in Germany and he remained respected as a remarkable strategist outside Germany.

On 13 May 1943 the Panzergruppe Afrika capitulated in Tunis.

9

The Message
Letters 5 October–7 December 1941

5 October 1941

. . .

Departure at 8 a.m. to the headquarters of an Italian division stationed at the Sollum front and inspection of the front line, back at 14.00 hours, covered with dust. Atmosphere at the font nonetheless refreshing. When we came back from our trip to the front, the new Chief of Staff, Bayerlein and I were surprised to find a message informing us that a certain Lieutenant Kraus had conducted an operation with some of his men during the night. They returned with an English vehicle and ten prisoners.

More sounds of engines and exchanges of gunfire in the air. Two English fighters were shot down near us. Sunday surprises. Tomorrow morning, Bayerlein and I will be leaving for the Tobruk front and Tuesday to the divisions. Wednesday, hunting with Colonel Knabe. Afterwards, I presume that I have to work in my office.

. . .

6 October 1941

. . .

Today, we visited the front at Tobruk. We chose an advanced spot offering an excellent view of the port and the town. The town has changed since my last visit. The harbour is full of wrecks. We counted twenty-eight.

Yesterday evening I received a letter from General Müller-Gebhard. Through his car accident some time ago he had missed his plane. He had to take another flight. Later, he learned that the plane he was to take in the first place had been shot down. He was lucky again.

We shot down five English fighters today. It happens now almost every day. Last night, I spent an hour in the shelter. When a plane bombed us again, I decided to go there.

. . .

11 October 1941

. . .

Yesterday, Colonel Bayerlein and I escorted a company of armoured vehicles to the east of Tobruk. It was exciting to take part in an operation. Then we advanced and this time accompanied tanks on the right. It was pretty to observe the exchange of gunshots, a real firework show. It all worked perfectly. It was so refreshing to take part in an operation. The English lost two bases to us, without great own losses. The English have run away. Negligible loot. The Italians moved in and occupied them. We advanced about 7 km. What surprised me is that the English artillery fired back so little. It was as if they wanted to keep concentrated on their defence until we got to the inner ring of their fortifications. What do they really want?

Yesterday, another bomb hit a vehicle of the Panzergruppe. Two officers died, like a few days ago. Yesterday, the reporter-photographer Eric Borchert was seriously injured. He was already been transferred out. I made arrangements at the personnel office to prolong his stay, because he did not want to leave us. In wartime, one has to let fate to take its course. One should not try to influence it.

. . .

12 October 1941

. . .

The situation has not changed around Tobruk. The English apparently accepted the loss of two bases. Strange. But their artillery fire on Sollum has inflicted significant losses on the Italians. At Sollum they took one of our outposts.

Today, thick fog delayed the start of our chase. But when the sun filtered through the mist, 6.30 hours, it became even more beautiful. I have only killed a female gazelle. I missed a male, although the distance between it and the car became shorter and shorter. For sure, I would have got it, if a sudden jolt had not stopped the car, which wouldn't start again. The best all-terrain vehicles are not strong enough to withstand these hunts for kilometre after kilometre at speeds of around 80 km per hour. We did not get the buck but, instead, we found Wüstefeld again, whom we had lost. He shot a cheetah.

. . .

13 October 1941,

My beloved! At the end of my birthday, which could not have better spent in the desert, all my thoughts are with you to thank you again for everything. But I do believe that we all will celebrate my birthday together next year. At the end of this day, I read my birthday letters in peace.

Tonight, planes dropped lots of bombs.

In the morning, at 6.45 hours, I left with Bayerlein for Tobruk. We stopped at Gambut having noticed Rommel's vehicle by the door. He explained his plans for the future. Then we followed him to the general meeting place. We inspected the first line of the front, on foot and by car, specifically the part that would be occupied today. The weather was extremely favourable. Very strong wind and sand coming from the south, blocking the line of sight for the English completely, and we were able to approach their lines without being noticed. The Italian troops were surprised seeing us, positioned far behind us.

16.00 hours: white tablecloth, Bayerlein, Wüstefeld and a military music corps, organised by Knabe. Excellent coffee, this time not salty, prepared by Pfistermeister with Peregrino. Pancakes with marmalade, delicious. Other guests came up to congratulate us, von Ziegler, Riemer and Sannow. I asked the leader of the music corps to play for us. We spent an agreeable time while the music played.

. . .

14 October 1941

. . .

Bayerlein really wants me to remain at my post. But I think that my transfer cannot be stopped any longer. After a certain time spent in Africa, the transfer of all officers becomes urgent and is necessary.

This morning at 9.00, my friend Lieutenant Köhler passed by just to wish me a happy birthday. He gave me two cakes prepared by the baker of his company who had constructed an oven using an oil drum. He concocts delicious cakes when the ingredients are available to him.

. . .

15 October 1941

. . .

Bayerlein asked me to prepare a conference on the Deutsches Afrika Korps from its beginnings to inform the new general-in-chief, Crüwell, whom we expect within the next few days. I am the only member of the staff who has been present in Africa from the very beginning.

Today, another special announcement: 560,000 Russian soldiers captured. Yet some believe that the war will drag on for a long time. Suddenly, the English have become very active here in Africa. Submarines are sighted from time to time. They may come; they will be met with a rebuff, as usual.

The day was calm and the planes did not come last night or so far today. General von Ravenstein wished me a happy birthday. I received a letter from Lieutenant Basilius at the military hospital in Athens. He thanked me for intervening on his behalf to get transport by car and plane to Athens, where his wounded leg was *not* amputated. It was highly timely. Rapid transport was essential if they hope to avoid amputation. This is what happens if we do not pay attention even to small injuries in this terrible region.

. . .

16 October 1941

. . .

A few moments ago, a special announcement informed us that our troops have occupied Odessa in southern Russia. But I do not believe that Stalin wishes to conclude an armistice. He hopes that we will not withstand the winter. I still firmly believe that the war will end next year. If only the Mediterranean was cleared of the English!

. . .

17 October 1941

It's bitter cold at night.

We were told that a small schooner would bring us vegetables and pigs from Greece. It seems that the English have got the cargo.

. . .

20 October 1941

. . .

Crüwell, the new general, is a kind and reassuring personality, a man of great distinction and authority. One can feel that he can be strict. He told me immediately that he had precise information about me: 'That you know it right away, the High Command of the Army appreciates you very much.' Crüwell assured me that he was pleased to have at his side an experienced aide de camp.

. . .

21 October 1941

. . .

The position of an adjutant with Crüwell has a greater importance than with Rommel, who called me only whom he had an order to give.

An aircraft circled above our heads for some time. Curious, I went outside. Precisely at this moment the plane dropped its bombs on Bardia, followed by grenades coming from the sea. It was the first time English warships shot at us. We will have to take it into account in future. Our coastal batteries responded and are still shooting, although the English are now silent for a while.

. . .

22 October 1941

. . .

During a lengthy discussion, Crüwell revealed that the personnel office in Berlin was very surprised that Rommel had done nothing to secure me as his adjutant to the Panzergruppe. Among other things he wanted to know Rommel's motives. I replied that I understood his position. Rommel considers it necessary to change members of his staff frequently. But it is also possible that my wish to be transferred to the front influenced his decision. Crüwell, quite surprised, asked me where I wanted to be transferred. 'I understand your wish and I take note. You will forgive me, but for now, you cannot leave this post. By the way, as my adjutant, you can, of course, come to see me at any time, even if I don't want to be disturbed.'

I write to you about it because it amuses me. How, after my time with Rommel, the position of an adjutant changes with a different person, more of a commanding general than Rommel who often went to the front during attacks, presenting himself more like a head of a commando rather than as a commanding general.

When Crüwell and I were in the area this morning, we observed all of a sudden thirty-nine English planes above us, which started dropping their bombs a little further away. Two German fighters encircled and attacked them. They shot one English plane. Two against thirty-nine, an uneven ratio. That's why they should only attack the one keeping itself on the sidelines. The insolence with which the English fly over us is difficult to take.

. . .

23 October 1941

. . .

Another air-raid warning in Bardia.

We heard explosions. First bombs, then artillery shelling of warships. But our coastal batteries have fired not without success. It is 1:15 hours now. Everything seems to be calm.

Bardia, 24 October 1941

. . .

It is only 21.45 hours but we have already been in the bunker. A plane dropped parachute flares so we expected shelling of warships, but we have received only one bomb. Crüwell told me today again that no member of the Afrika Korps looked as well and healthy as I do. I do not look like someone who has been in Africa for such a long time. (I can only repeat my usual comment: 'Alas!') But, I am fine.

. . .

26 October 1941

. . .

As the previous nights had been much disturbed, we moved straight to the desert after dinner. The right decision. Bombing began at nightfall. At the same time, our planes attacked the English ships. We observed one of them burning, while the other ships covered Bardia with particularly intense shelling. After each bombing and attack, we need to repair our lodgings and offices. Our switchboard (one of the few services remaining at Bardia) got a direct hit. Thank God, we had only one slightly injured.

. . .

27 October 1941

. . .

Cooperation among the staff under Crüwell is developing very well, actually better than before. But the new general demands far more attention than Rommel. That takes much time.

In the coming period, probably, as a result of the current situation relocation of staff might become necessary, but only for a limited time.

A speedboat tried to approach the coast. Our coastal battery fired at it at a distance of 500 m. The boat changed course. I scolded the battery. Instead of letting the boat approach to sink it, they missed it at the distance of 500 m.

. . .

28 October 1941

My beloved, you will be angry that your husband did not write to you yesterday. It was not possible. I was too busy. Yesterday morning, at 7.00 hours I started out with Crüwell to attend an exercise of military sappers. Lunch at Walter's. Then stop at the artillery, back at 16.40 and at 17.00 hours with Rommel, back at 19.45 and at 20.00 hours, night quarters in the desert. And the day was over.

In the desert, aircraft don't disturb us. We hear their engines and bombs shaking the ground in Bardia but they don't affect us.

. . .

30 October 1941

. . .

Yesterday afternoon, I had a very pleasant and interesting trip with Crüwell to the Halfaya Pass, disputed by English and German troops.

Given the time needed for our letters to arrive, we should already consider whether we should continue writing to each other, whether you should still send me packages, for example. You will only receive this letter around 15 November. And I shall receive your answer as late as end of November or early December, at the latest on 10 December; I intend to leave for Rome on the 12th and be in Gera on the 14th or 15th. I shall probably have to go to Berlin before Christmas to see the personnel office.

Almost every night, I listen to Lili Marleen on Radio Athens. Everyone listens. Initially, I did not realise how it might be a kind of meeting point for the thoughts and feelings we have for those who are dear to us in Germany. Now, I know our thoughts come together when this song is on the air.

My impression is that you have finally decided to come to Rome. It would be wonderful!

. . .

31 October 1941

. . .

We reviewed last night, Crüwell, Bayerlein and I, the best way to mark Rommel's anniversary 15 November. He will celebrate his fiftieth birthday and his twenty-fifth wedding anniversary at the same time. We are giving him a carpet, and a letter written by Crüwell. Crüwell wants me to hand everything over. I am not terribly keen on doing it, but Rommel will be happy to see me.

I hope that in spite of your difficulties you always have enough to eat.

The day before yesterday I received a letter from the personnel office announcing my coming transfer. Crüwell refuses to let me go before Easter 1942. The office staff promised it to him. For my part, I had to promise him not to undertake from my side any personal initiative and to find him a valid successor ready for my transfer. He assured me he would intervene so that I get transferred to a post to suit me.

Your missing letters didn't arrive again yesterday. A plane has probably disappeared.

. . .

2 November 1941

. . .

Yesterday, I accompanied General Crüwell from six o'clock in the morning until the afternoon. We assisted at very interesting manoeuvre that showed us how it should not be done from a military point of view.

Bayerlein and I were enjoying a roasted gazelle at Crüwell's place, when bombing started again that lasted until 2.00. I heard the noise in the far distance. Every day in the evening my bags are prepared for the night ready to leave for the desert. After our planes sank a cruiser, we don't receive any shelling from the seaside at the moment. My evenings are not at leisure any more. Now I accompany Crüwell on his evening strolls. Before, we played cards with the former chief of staff. Work is more demanding for me now, because Crüwell includes me more in his tasks. Now I rarely do the jobs of an adjutant. Professionally, I am very pleased about it. Now all we have to do is take Tobruk, followed by my taking leave, and the world will be in order.

Yesterday, I received seven letters, including one from an officer who fell ill in Germany; it is often the case that those leaving Africa in good health becoming sick with dysentery and hepatitis back in Germany.

Thank God Crüwell sleeps well. Hence he is never in a bad mood in the morning. Currently, the situation here seems to be by far more agreeable than in Russia. The latest news is good again. Our fronts are quiet for the moment. For us, taking Tobruk is the *conditio sine qua non* of this campaign.

The English seem to accept the loss of terrain which we took about ten days ago. In four weeks, they will have to accept further losses of terrain.

. . .

3 November 1941

. . .

Yesterday, I gave a lecture on the campaign in North Africa so far. Crüwell thanked me in a very kind way and congratulated me. The others appeared to be satisfied as well, for I am the only one to have taken part in the campaign from the very beginning. Now Crüwell and Bayerlein would like to have a presentation on the fighting around Tobruk. They asked Wüstefeld to be the next to prepare a lecture on the *Panzerschlacht* [tank battle] of Sollum.

. . .

I received a long letter and a little book, *Your Horse and You*, from General Müller-Gebhard yesterday. It's nice on his part and rather unexpected. I don't deserve so much attention.

What would your parents say if we do not go to Klein Silkow for Christmas in this beautiful winter season? They will certainly be sad. They would miss our two sons. Do you think that we could extend our trip to Berlin and spend two days in Klein Silkow after my talks?

Crüwell was surprised that I always get up so early in the morning and that I don't give the impression of having suffered of the harsh strains of the campaign up to now. Our life here, almost without alcohol, is healthy.

. . .

4 November 1941

My beloved, I went hunting at 3.00 hours. Back at 15.00, I found four letters from you on the table, numbered 76, 77, 78 and 79. I am still miss your letters of 10 to 17 October, numbers 63 to 69. I am delighted to have news from you again. So, you don't want to come to Rome? It is a great pity, but just before Christmas you will have not enough time to prepare everything for Christmas and you don't want to leave our two sons alone during Advent. I am slowly getting ready for leave.

Crüwell came to see me in my office yesterday afternoon. He smoked a cigarette. He solemnly promised to let me go on leave. But, of course, I can only request it if the situation permits it: once Tobruk is taken then I know that my leave can be approved.

Knabe just called me. The English bombed a munitions depot near his camp.

I was still in Bardia, and I had just finished writing letters when the first bombs fell. I ran as fast as I could into the shelter. Just at this moment two parachute flares opened above my office and the bombs were already falling at a distance of only 500 m. Thank God, the full moon has ended now, but eight days will still have to pass before we have calm again.

. . .

5 November 1941

. . .

My beloved, this morning I had all the peace needed to resolve the pile of work problems on my desk. I am spending generally a lot of time trying to get the signatures of Bayerlein and Crüwell for letters and documents that I have prepared for them, as the planning of a new attack on Tobruk requires many meetings and instructions all day long.

I'm thinking of having a second leave at Easter 1942, at the latest Pentecost. What kind of events still unknown will we experience by then? It's wiser and more appropriate to establish a programme only on a day-to-day basis. The heat today was painful, 55° to 60°C, I think, brought about by an unpleasant wind from the south with traces of sirocco, not as disagreeable as last May, but persistent. The newcomers are down, while we, the veterans, although not used to this furnace heat either, are less affected. That's all, my beloved, I lack energy today.

6 November 1941

. . .

Yesterday evening, we had our traditional visit: a plane greeted us with a few bombs. I went to bed early, but it was very hot. Around 0:30 hours I was awakened from cold. Which gruesome region!

This morning I attended a training exercise, extremely well organised by General Sümmermann. All commanders were present. I was glad to see them again. There were many new faces. In four weeks, I shall be travelling home!

. . .

7 November 1941

My beloved, Crüwell told me today that I could make you happy, that I can have eight days more in December to meet the personnel office in Berlin. It will be necessary that I go to see this department every two months to discuss personnel matters of the divisions. He arranged it with the division commanders, putting their trust in me. And he added verbally: 'If I offer you an opportunity to see your wife more often, you might stay longer with me.'

Today was an important day. Almost all the commanders, accompanied by other officers of our troops, a total of fifty-eight people, came to attend a wargame from 9.00 to 12.30, excellent, followed by lunch at our mess, preceded by a photo session, music corps, set up by me. The mess functioned perfectly. Menu: consommé, canned fish, soup of canned green beans, cheese sandwiches, coffee, all accompanied by red and white wine, cigars, cigarettes. The tables were prepared very well. After lunch, meetings, first of the officers, followed by the division commanders. Crüwell has repeatedly thanked everybody, which was different to Rommel's way – he was never been able to utter such words. He is a real character, and I believe the commanders share my opinion. I hope that the Crüwell–Bayerlein duo will continue for a long time.

Last night, quite late, I had to preside over the funeral of Captain Pistorius, Navy Department, whom I did not know. Captain von Amsberg, a former pastor, improvised a few words adapted to the circumstance in front of the tomb. Pistorius, married with two sons at the front, a third still in school, en route to Bardia to inspect the port, collided with an Italian truck. Did he come for that from Berlin? It's really tragic.

Colonel Knabe and Colonel Mickl were very cheerful, as I had never seen them before. Really, here in Africa everything is different! Commanders, unknown to me before, become very close and familiar in minutes – thanks to the dirt and the desert which we all share. That makes us all more equal, no one is better off than the other.

. . .

8 November 1941

. . .

No sooner I had gone to bed English planes had arrived but left again. Finally, a single plane approached at low altitude. Suddenly, I saw sparks splashing in front of my window, door panels, dust; everything flew around, everything upside down. Everywhere, dust, dirt, debris. In the office, files covered by rubble, doors torn off their frames, and so on. In Wüstefeld's house was worse. Ceilings and part of the walls had collapsed. In the mess and in the church, ceilings and walls down, at the general's place, the same everywhere. Today it became clear, it was not a simple bomb, but a special bomb, the blast of which destroys everything within a certain perimeter. The bomb detonated 150 m from my office.

The houses close to the detonation and around me are no longer recognisable or habitable. Afterwards the aircraft returned several times that I sought refuge in the shelter three times. Tonight, we went back to the desert for security reasons, and intend to continue doing so. I suppose that the English reconnaissance aircraft spotted a lot of movement around and in the houses of Bardia (commanders' wargame, meetings). No losses to be feel sorry about.

Crüwell told me that I could leave for Berlin eight days after the operation on Tobruk. My departure would be then much earlier than I had expected.

9 November 1941

. . .

At 5.00, I got up to go hunting with Knabe. Until noon, we rode in the desert back and forth and saw not one gazelle, only two hares, one of which disappeared in a wadi. Of a flock of wild chickens, we killed three. I gave one to Crüwell.

Daylight after 6.00, the sun was shining, but then the sky clouded again accompanied by a wind coming from northwest. Despite a pullover and a thick grey coat, we were cold. You probably won't understand it, but for us it was really cold. I am a little afraid of December in Germany, thinking of my leave. I shall stay near the heating or just stay in bed. You can bring my meals to my bed to conserve my strength. Worries! But in four weeks, I might be at home already, my beloved, if you don't come to Rome.

Bardia received some more bombs. The windows and doors of my office were flung again open by the blast. All the cables were damaged by the bombs.

Today, it is already 10 November. I think that both of us will go to Berlin in our days in December. Ideally, you will pick me up in Rome and take me back.

. . .

Bardia, 11 November 1941

. . .

Colonel Bayerlein and I went further to the front to seek another location for the command. We probably went a little bit too far. We were happy with a spot offering a large view over the area outside Tobruk when some shells exploded in front of us. We quickly left.

I mentioned to Bayerlein that Crüwell might have been sorry that none of us were present in Bardia last night. He replied, 'Especially that you weren't there. He appreciates you so much!'

Yesterday, Bayerlein sent a proposal to Berlin to appoint me lieutenant colonel, endorsed by Crüwell. In addition, the Panzergruppe intends that all officers present for some time in Africa should get a promotion. I agree with that. My appointment to the rank of lieutenant colonel might be faster in that case.

Today, Lieutenant Richter returned from leave, well rested. He was glad to be back in Africa.

I received some sad news: our pharmacist, Dandert, died while returning from leave. His plane crashed in Serbia.

You will come with me to Berlin? I won't stop asking. You could already look for a train leaving Gera for Berlin.

The plan to take Tobruk has complicated everything here. It is a pity that I can't speak about it, but I will do it later.

. . .

12 November 1941

. . .

This morning, I left with Crüwell and Bayerlein to attend a very interesting and instructive exercise of the Italians, perfectly commanded. Everything was excellent. It was a manoeuvre with real fire. Good moral and strategy. We could not do better. I am only afraid that, as soon as the English begin to shoot at them, their morale will fail. A plethora of officers came as spectators. After this manoeuvre, I joined our new command post. From there, I observed an attack by Stukas on Tobruk. I do not think that there is a coin left that has not been bombed.

Which hotel shall we take in Berlin? I vote for the Excelsior. Frost will deter the British from bombing Berlin precisely on those two nights.

13 November 1941

. . .

Although departure from our camp in the desert is set at 7 a.m., I go to Bardia earlier for washing. The dust of the desert sticks to the body.

Due to a car crash, I was unable to participate in Walter's war exercise. Alas, it was as I feared. Boring and hesitant. Late afternoon, Crüwell and I discussed at great length the course of the exercise. He respects Walter a lot as gentleman, but he could not get on with the presentation given by his division. Today, according to Crüwell, the cautious side of Walter's character became palpable. He feels a lot for him and is willing to help him, if necessary. I am very happy to be part of the staff of someone thinking so decently.

. . .

14 November 1941

. . .

Bayerlein wanted to know the other day what choice he should put as a priority into his proposal for my appointment to lieutenant colonel. I thought first to mention panzer, but in the end I opted for a reconnaissance unit or a motorised battalion. This would please me more, recalling the cavalry, and it does not demand too much technical knowledge.

Yesterday, Crüwell repeated that he would not let me go for the time being.

Another reserve lieutenant (a former judge) has been declared unfit for military service: kidney stones, another has hepatitis. Here, the diseases do not stop. I always have to make sure to have some officers at hand. The drain on officers is too high. Because of our losses on the Eastern front, we will get no reinforcements. Lieutenant Colonel von Wechmar, commander of a reconnaissance unit, was finally declared unfit to live in the tropics. Don't worry I'm still fine!

The situation remains unchanged, although the English are very active. They are everywhere. But it will pass soon. News from Russia is rare. Something is going on. In any case, it is unfortunate that the climate there in November is now a hindrance.

Good morning! The night was calm, although one could hear powerful bombing in the far distance.

I hope to be in Gera in three weeks.

. . .

16 November 1941

. . .

Heading for an invitation to dinner at Walter's, I was delayed by the general-in-chief. I took the road a quarter of an hour too late. I needed those fifteen minutes to find the diversion of the Via Balbia leading to the camp of the 15th Panzer Division. It is always extremely difficult to find the right path at nightfall because of the multiple tracks, traces of vehicles, junctions and bifurcations. Walter has constructed a first-class mess, well equipped, beautifully situated at the top of a hill overlooking a wadi close to the seaside. The menu was excellent: fish, rice, grilled liver, spinach, omelette, red wine followed by coffee, beer and gin, and later whisky-and-soda. No one was permitted by the host to leave. On my return, late at night, I went to the Panzergruppe where Bayerlein and I intended to meet at six o'clock in the morning to go hunting. Neither Bayerlein nor his aide turned up.

Back at Bardia, I learned that Bayerlein was unable to leave because of a violent air raid between 3 and 5 a.m. Some fifty aircraft overflew Bardia in tight formation so that two of them collided and crashed. They hurled firebombs and explosives. It was our way of hunting gazelles!

You ask if the letters missing mean that a plane has crashed. Generally, we are not informed. As not long ago soldiers on leave died in a plane crash, I know by coincidence that on 23 October, an Italian aircraft with twenty-three soldiers on board crashed. They are all dead. It will often happen that a plane does not arrive.

Have you learned about the success of our submarines in the Mediterranean? It's fabulous! Now, nothing can leave or enter Tobruk.

Tomorrow afternoon, Crüwell and I go to see Rommel to wish happy birthday to him. Did I write that the information on the silver wedding anniversary of Rommel was false? A rumour from the Panzergruppe.

. . .

17 November 1941

My beloved, I am again very well. Yesterday I had caught cold, I mentioned it in my last letter. It worsened toward the evening and I could hardly see ahead, all my bones were hurting. I was afraid of falling ill. Fifteen days before my leave! In bed by nine, two glasses of hot white wine, and this morning everything was gone, refreshed and feeling healthy. It surprised me.

This morning we witnessed an armoured manoeuvre at Walter's. It was pretty lame. During the comments that followed, Walter criticised the operations very much. Yet, in the end, it will affect the reputation of the entire division. I believe that during our next movements against Tobruk, the division will attack differently. A good strategy would put the English on their knees. It is good that our submarines operate effectively in the Mediterranean. They will ensure that nobody can escape from Tobruk.

Today, for the first time since I arrived in Africa, it's pouring down. When I arrived in the vicinity of my wadi, a few moments ago, I heard a roar, and suddenly a mountain torrent came towards me. Two of my collaborators were already in their tent when this torrent, large, 2 metres deep, flowed under their beds.

The night was calm.

19 November 1941

. . .

No sooner were we installed for a little early dinner in Lieutenant Albrecht's grotto, after a cocktail and having finished a delicious entrée, than we were informed about an attack on us by the English. We had to abandon everything and to return at high speed to the staff.

War was back again, all of a sudden.

It is too early for me to give you details. But sure: the English will be rebuffed again.

It is important that the headquarters move as soon as possible out of Bardia. You cannot imagine the difficulties that accumulate. And even now not everything is on a level as it should have been. Everybody without distinction, whether sections, officers, troops has installed themselves in Bardia, in the wadis and canyons as in peacetime. It's incomprehensible! How many times I had told them that the General Staff must be ready to move at any moment! We were lucky, though, because we regularly left Bardia for the night. Thus, we could repair some breakdowns. It is really unfortunate that the capable commander of Bardia was on leave and his representative quite incompetent. Many vehicles remained in the work-shop and many other things had been found out. In addition newly moved officers without any experience have complicated the task.

If the English had advanced yesterday, they could have captured half of the staff. But they haven't. A prisoner told us incredible details. Colonel Bayerlein interrogated him twice. The situation is such that it can change every five minutes.

Crüwell has gone to the front. I would have liked to go with him, but I had to take care of the group here. Bayerlein wanted my presence here.

We will see clearer about noon, on Crüwell's return after his discussions with the Panzergruppe.

It is for sure that the English engaged this attack to divert our attention from Tobruk. Rommel, back since yesterday afternoon, had a nice surprise.

Yesterday, it did not stop raining on and off. The desert has become a difficult terrain to use, vehicles getting stuck. The rain doesn't soak into the ground. There are puddles everywhere. The valleys are flooded. To the west of Tobruk, the bridge was swept away. The stores and canteen were severely damaged. Also our aircraft cannot take off. The ground has become too soft; it is waterlogged. English planes came overnight. They have certainly improved runways in Egypt.

. . .

Our officers and others have learned to swim in their wadis overnight. Their cases were washed away by the rain, and so on. Confusion everywhere. I received three of your letters, soaked, but still legible.

We are really in a terrible region. I can only repeat it!

Today's events were different from those still imagined yesterday. Do not yet worry about the possibility of delaying my leave. For the moment, there is no reason for it. The English will again abandon the field and the programme will proceed as planned.

Crüwell and Bayerlein are great: calm, objective and kind. Don't worry if one day you can't receive my letters. It just means that I haven't found a way to write and send it.

. . .

23 November 1941

. . .

A few words so that you know that I am fine. Lately, I couldn't find the time to send you some lines. The day before yesterday, I wrote to you from Bardia. I gave this letter to Panzergruppe. But since then, not a single moment of peace.

We left Bardia in haste. After that, we moved into a wadi, functional and beautiful. Since yesterday morning we've been on the move again, now here, now there, permanently encircled by English troops who arrive en masse on all sides. They deploy an enormous number of tanks.

We are living critical times. The question is: 'to be or not to be' for the Deutsches Afrika Korps. The extremely skilful leadership of Crüwell and the impeccable work of Bayerlein will probably guarantee success ultimately.

The fact is that we didn't know, didn't hear anything about the fact, that the English would suddenly appear in such enormous strength! They brought five divisions (it is said that they were considerably weakened by fighting). They manoeuvred skilfully. But how is it possible that 500 tanks advance unnoticed through the desert to Benghazi? You witness a mystery.

We can only explain the advance by the fact that Rommel was solely focused on the assault of Tobruk, and did not want to believe any other information. The English knew, of course, of our intention to attack Tobruk and started the operation in a final attempt to save Tobruk and, after our defeat, to reconquer Libya. But they are mistaken. Our situation is excellent. The Tobruk front line held despite strong assaults coming from the fortifications. On the outside, even though they came very close, English troops have not been able to enter the town. But fighting the day before yesterday and yesterday, facing English superiority on all sides, has not been easy.

A few moments ago, I spoke with a doctor who was a prisoner for two days. He has been well treated. But the ordinary soldiers stole everything in his pockets: money, wallet, everything disappeared. During the onslaught of German panzers this morning, he managed to make the English guards his own prisoners.

The day passes quickly. I still hope that we will be able to try a coup and take Tobruk. It is very optimistic, perhaps too optimistic. I know. The problem of supply is there all the time afresh.

I am fine, my beloved. Dealing with Crüwell is excellent. His strategy is clear. I have no news of Wim, but Walter is fine.

I hope I can go on leave in ten days, if not a few days later.

. . .

***

In 1941, I was seven years old, and my brother eight. The war had become for us a reality to which I myself, despite the absence of my father, became more or less habituated. After his departure at the end of July to meet Rommel in Wiener Neustadt to return with him to the front in North Africa, my life resumed its course in Gera. Holidays were finished, we returned to Gera and I attended the elementary school. My father was absent, like the fathers of most of my classmates.

After beginning the war against the Soviet Union the war situation figured more and more in the daily lives of us schoolchildren. Suddenly teachers were missing, and we had fewer lessons, which we obviously welcomed with joy, according to our age misjudging the seriousness of the situation. Our discussions in class mentioned the war as a fact, but not more. The conversations that we had about the war tended only to revolve around where our fathers were fighting, in Russia, in the Balkans or in Africa. The majority of my classmates' fathers were fighting in Russia. I do not remember hearing any of my classmates saying that his father was in Libya.

I knew that the fighting in North Africa was more serious again after the November and probably guessed that the situation had worsened. Rare were the letters my mother received in these days. This lack of mail tormented her. She remained rather vague in her answers when we asked her about the contents of the letters that arrived very irregularly since the beginning of the British counter-offensive and she just repeated the information that she had heard on the radio or from friends whose husbands were also fighting in Africa.

Towards the end of November 1941 only a few letters arrived; the ones that did were often brief and hastily written. My mother grew more and more concerned. We naturally saw that she – as always – wrote her letters daily, restless, filling many pages, as if she wanted to get rid of her concerns, still hoping to see him at Christmas. So she wrote to him every day, at the same hour, in the late afternoon sitting at her husband's black desk. She addressed the envelope, provided it with a stamp, and went to the letter box at the street corner. One day she commented that opening a second front in the East would be beyond Germany's means especially with the approaching winter, picking up remarks from my father's letters where he dreaded the long winters in the East, a concern that came up several times in his letters.

1 December 1941

My beloved, tomorrow, it will be fourteen days since we went on the move. I could only write to you once. I simply lacked time and a break. So it is, when you are continuously engaged in hard fighting day and night or encircled by English troops. We had many, very tough moments. Very often, we thought that it had gone our way, but new English forces arrived that we had to beat.

The English, South Africans, Indians and New Zealanders are fighting with bravery and are tenacious. They escape us at the last minute; resurface somewhere at our side, always superior in numbers and equipment. They have not only fresh troops, but also excellent equipment, vehicles and weapons. They are well supplied. On the other hand, we have, for example, today again, as happened very often, after three days no fresh food any more. We live mostly on loot taken from the English: corned beef, chocolate, cigarettes, canned butter. This is not too bad. We are hoping that our mobile kitchen trailer with its stock is still somewhere in the area, so we can have hot dishes from time to time. It's the same with water. Today is the second time that I've been able to shave for the past two weeks. Water is used only for hand washing and shaving. We are all filthy, but all in the same boat, trying to pass these difficult moments in this area.

Those whose cars were stolen, destroyed or burned are in a very uncomfortable situation. This is my case. Pfistermeister transported some wounded in my car. He wanted to bring them to our main first aid station. On the way, one of those many English patrols in the area took him prisoner. I haven't yet seen him. According to the information I got, he will be returned, but, of course, without my car and my bag. Everything remained in English hands. I miss very much my thick, grey military coat, as it is very cold at night. I guess that Pfistermeister when he comes back might have already got certain things from the English.

The battle seems to end. Yesterday and today, we have taken a large number of prisoners and took to the enemy a lot of vehicles, but it does not exhaust their reserves. The fighting could continue for a long time. I hope and am confident that I will be with you at Christmas.

My beloved, we have experienced a lot and were at the same time lucky. The war in the desert, which has not been so intense until now, is worse than the one in Europe. In addition there is the superiority of the British air force that constantly bombards us. Today, we saw the German fighters again for the first time. The English planes don't show up one at a time, but always twenty or more. Aerial bombardment is worse than artillery fire.

But, in short, I am fine. My wounds will heal soon. Only a flesh wound. Colonel Mickl is fine. Not much is left of his regiment. Colonel Knabe is well. Walter, as a person, is very brave, but he is not very good at commanding panzers. Crüwell or Rommel don't always approve of what he does. Today, they want him to return to Germany now. Instead of him they sent back his adjutant.

Let me conclude, my beloved. I hope to be able to send you this letter and that you will receive it without any problem.

I hope that you do not worry too much because of the Army Reports that do not speak too well about us. By the way, General von Ravenstein was captured.

. . .

On 9 December 1941, influenza was rampant in Gera and all three of us, my mother, my brother and I, had fever. We were all in bed. The postman rang at the door. Herta, our maid, brought my mother one of the few letters that my father had been able to write during the last weeks. The letter showed his concern about the war in North Africa more clearly than ever before, and the difficulty of fighting British supremacy. My mother came to us and briefly reported the essence of it, without hiding her deep concern. The letter was ten days old.

29 November 1941

My beloved! Commander Skubin just passes by to get our mail, hoping that it can be sent.

I am fine.

We have some dramatic days behind us and will have probably others. The English have a force four times bigger than ours. They are very brave, but we are better, and we will have ended this sparring in short time.

Three days ago, I was slightly injured. A piece of shrapnel hit my right temple. I am fine. I have no complaints.

Colonel Mickl after a captivity of two and a half days came back to us. He fought with courage and will hopefully be awarded with Knight's Cross of the Iron Cross. Wüstefeld together with some members of his staff were taken prisoner, as well as Pfistermeister with my car. My bag is lost. But our morale is good.

My permission will be slightly delayed. However, I will be with you at Christmas. I hope you are well.

The next day, 10 December, it was worse. We were all three even more poorly. It was one of those typical days in December. It was grey and wet. The house was poorly heated. Coal shortage. The war began to affect everything, colouring daily life.

It was between nine and ten o'clock. The doorbell rang. Herta went to open it. Standing there was one of my mother's friends, the wife of Colonel Heidkämper. The Heidkämpers lived upstairs, and their children played with us every day. Mrs Heidkämper's arms held a large bouquet of flowers. She wanted to see my mother.

I heard whispering, a few words, then the heavy front door was closed. Footsteps towards my parents' bedroom. Then I heard a few words, Mrs Heidkämper's voice, not her usually clear voice. Silence. Again some words. Then I heard more steps in the hall.

My mother told me later that she had felt a huge weight on her when she saw the big bouquet of lilies in her friend's arms, as she stood without a word on the threshold of her room, looking at her. Her husband had been killed in action, she said. Yesterday. She was in a way prepared, had expected somehow the news, although she always feared it, and felt finally that she was not prepared for it at all. Moments later, my mother came into our room to announce us that we would not see our father again. Her words were sober, her eyes dry. It was a brief moment, but poignant. And silence fell upon us. My mother informed her father-in-law and her parents, who invited her to come and spend Christmas with them. The exchanges were short. She rang up the wife of her cousin, General Neumann-Silkow, who was killed in action the same day, 9 December 1941, some hours earlier.

After 10 December I still imagined that everything was just fantasy, the news was false. The Afrika Korps could have been mistaken, as I did not know the circumstances of his death. Moreover, letters of my father continued to arrive. They were letters he had written before his death, rushed, restless, somehow desperate, fighting against British supremacy.

On 13 December the postman delivered the following letter. My father had written it on 3 December, six days before his death. The envelope, stamps, everything was as it used to be, but the text of the letter was different, just a few lines, disturbing.

3 December 1941

. . .

I finally got chance to send you some lines. I am fine. Pfistermeister is back, but without my suitcase etc., it remains with the English. I live on spoils.

I think I can say more soon. Love Jochen

Two days later, another letter arrived.

4 December 1941

. . .

I think of you today. I am fine, but the English fired at us at night and we were heavily shelled. Taking advantage of the full moon, we were constantly shelled and exposed to attacks at low altitude. We are dug in a hole. As my beautiful car has fallen into the hands of the English, Pfistermeister organised a small car for me, an Opel. An interim solution. I hope to have a better car soon, more spacious. Pfistermeister takes great pains to make life as comfortable as possible for me. I am surprised and I don't quite understand how he was able to bring my toiletries and my briefcase from his captivity, but all the letters and other documents are burned. I shall miss some of them.

Our field kitchen with its provisions has returned. We will again have hot meals, wonderful during the current chilly weather.

Today, I wrote to Mrs Wüstefeld, Mrs von Amsberg and Mrs von Sannow, among others. These personal letters had the same message (the husband won't be returning, because he's been captured, killed, whatever).

At the moment, I don't think I can leave here soon. Of course, the most important battle is won, but the English continue to fight with tenacity. Nevertheless, I still hope to see you for Christmas. There are still three weeks, but you do as you would prefer to do. If you want to go to Klein Silkow, I will join you there. Certainly not within the next ten days. You will be informed by radio of the exact day of my meeting in Berlin. That's why I won't send you my best wishes for Christmas amid the bombardments and as the situation is still confused, I don't like to think about Christmas. In a few days, the situation will have changed. It is changing every hour.

Walter, Mickl, Wim and Knabe are well. I don't know their current positions. We are scattered between Tobruk and Bardia.

My injury is healed, I have only a plaster. So you see that I am fine. After having lost weight a little during the first two weeks, I am putting on weight again. We eat a lot now, whenever we get the chance.

Two days later: another envelope arrived – two days before his death.

7 December 1941

My beloved! Behind me, someone said it was the second Sunday of Advent. Making such an observation in the midst of a war, and especially at the heart of battle like those that we are now experiencing, is strange, neither I nor my colleagues realised that before.

The war in the desert is completely different. The English fight remarkably well. Their artillery is especially effective. It threatens us from all sides. We had to change our position several times to avoid artillery shooting. Here in a desert which provides no shelter or cover, it has a very different effect on the troops, particularly morale.

Again we were inundated twice by waves of shelling. Today, they are tracking us particularly.

Rommel has just arrived. This is a very difficult and hard time for the command as we have not become stronger by the continuing fighting, now over three weeks. The losses of the troops are still tolerable compared to the previous greatest battle success which has not been decisive. The losses of the English are much higher. But they are stronger than us, both in numbers and equipment. The enemy is superior in many ways.

English vehicles relaced our cars which we had lost during the fighting. We are short of weapons. I think, I am convinced, that this will only be temporary. Everything possible will be done to bring us quickly what we are lacking. Refreshments and other deliveries are coming, despite enormous obstacles. Thus, we did not have any particular concerns.

My beloved, I am fine. But I think I have to hint discreetly that we should not count on leave at Christmas. Despite the intensive artillery fire, there won't be a decisive outcome today. I don't think so. I rather believe that we will have to fight for some time, perhaps weeks. One day the English will crumble if we cannot beat them decisively. Even if they receive sufficient supplies, at some point it will stop on their side.

The morale of the troops is excellent. All are conscious that we live at a critical time, a time rich in events and experiences.

Yesterday evening, Walter was seriously wounded in the lower jaw by shrapnel. Immediately after receiving this news, I wanted to see him, but he had been evacuated. I could only send a message by radio to the Panzergruppe to transport him immediately to Athens by plane. They say that his life is not in danger, but his recovery will take a lot of time.

At the level of commanders, the losses are impressive. Ravenstein in captivity and now Walter wounded. No news from General Sümmermann. General Crüwell and the Chief of Staff, Colonel Bayerlein, provide full command of the German Afrika Korps. In the most dramatic moments, it is a pleasure to see them acting with great authority. I hope that this letter will reach you during the coming two weeks, arriving at Christmas.

Have a beautiful Christmas and think a little of me as I think of you. But at this very moment, I am still hoping to arrive in time for Christmas. If this is not possible, I shall be one of the first to leave afterwards. Don't be sad, if I can't come: in that case I shall arrive in January, and we all will celebrate your birthday.

As I do not have enough time to write other letters, could you write to your parents in Klein Silkow and to my father and tell them that I am fine?

Epilogue

Two weeks passed without message from the Afrika Korps. It was necessary to get used to the fact that there would be no letters any more coming from Africa. The Christmas holidays had begun a few days before. We left for Klein Silkow to spend the holidays with our grandparents. The trip was long, a whole day. In three phases: first from Gera to Berlin; after a short stopover in the capital to Stolp, and finally arrival at a small station serving several villages in the countryside.

In all the railway compartments we took, nobody talked. Was it out of respect and discretion of this young widow dressed in black and her two children or did our presence remind them of the general situation, of the war, the effects of which were beginning to be felt in Germany, by rationing of certain foods, the first bombing raids on German towns, the decreasing number of military successes? When we changed station in the centre of Berlin, loaded with luggage, we could see the ruins caused by British aerial bombardment.

My grandparents' house was warm. Tiled fireplaces and stoves were lit everywhere. The staff had piled pieces of wood, of beech, oak, birch and pine that came directly from the forests. Only the long dark corridors were unheated. Outside, it was freezing cold; long winters are characteristic in this region, part of the former German eastern provinces. Siberian cold, as it was generally called, mountains and valleys, forests and fields disappeared under metres of snow.

Preparations for Christmas followed their course in 1941, as every year in Klein Silkow. Activities in the kitchen, the moving of furniture in the dining room, pine branches everywhere, the decoration of the Christmas tree delivered by the forest warden, the preparation of small tables for presents, decorated with small pine branches, smells of honey and cinnamon on all floors, an impromptu visitor could not have guessed what a profound pain the war had inflicted on my grandparents by the loss of their son-in-law and of their nephew, on their daughter, on this family.

That year, the atmosphere was less joyful, grim and sad. The loss of two members of the family that everyone liked, dying the same day in North Africa, my father and my uncle, plunged the house into a deep grief that united family, staff and the village as well. At the same time, they all knew that life continued: estate management and animal care demanded their share of attention. The annual meeting with the workers and their families on Christmas Eve late afternoon followed its traditional course: listening to my grandmother reading the Bible, singing together the traditional carols, while looking at the Christmas tree with its burning white candles. The discrete sympathy expressed by the workers and their families to my mother seemed to do her well. She knew everyone, and they all knew her.

After Christmas, the pain came back, mercilessly, in that house, in normal times full of joy and activity. On 31 December, around noon, the postman delivered to my mother an envelope from North Africa. The envelope had the handwriting of a stranger.

9 December 1941

My beloved! The division has announced that Walter is dead. Immediately afterwards, I sent you a radio message hoping that you would get it quite soon. I hope that you likewise received my first message to inform you that Walter was wounded. I am deeply shocked that he did not survive his injury. Besides the lower jaw injury, he had received a neck injury. I told you that he was immediately evacuated. In fact, he only came to Derna, because he couldn't be transported by air to Athens or Catania.

Those who knew him and had him as commander-in-chief of division deeply regret his death. My beloved, you are the first to receive this sad news and unfortunately you have the duty and heavy task to deliver the news to his family. How will Margarete receive this news? Her children? It's too sad. His funeral has certainly taken place today. We still have no details about it. There's no point in going there, in one hour it will be dark. It's 200 km to Derna and I do not think that I would succeed alone. So I couldn't even be present at his funeral.

As soon as the situation improves, I shall go to Derna and pray at his grave. It will be similar to that of General von Prittwitz at the military cemetery and possibly improved later.

. . .

His aide found this letter on his temporary desk in his tent the day of his death, 9 December 1941. It was unfinished. My father was called away. Major Hans-Joachim Schraepler was buried in Derna between General Walter Neumann-Silkow and General Max Sümmermann.

December 1941 was a black month for Panzergruppe Afrika, losing General Major Max Sümmermann, commander of 90th Light Infantry Division, who fell on 10 December 1941, Major Hans-Joachim Schraepler and General Major Walter Neumann-Silkow, commander of 15th Panzer Division, who died on 9 December 1941, the same day as my father, his cousin by marriage.

Later all three commanders were transferred to a memorial close to Tobruk. It is located south of the port, on top of a hill overlooking the town, the desert and the sea. It was erected after World War II in honour of the German soldiers, more than 6,000, who lost their lives in North Africa. The square shape with four massive towers at the corners and built with stone from the region recalls a castle of the Middle Ages. The names of the soldiers are inscribed on bronze plaques. In the inner courtyard four angels support a large cauldron.

After the war, friends told my mother that Rommel reckoned 9 December 1941 as the saddest day of the Libya–Egypt campaign.

My father died before Germany declared war on the United States of America on 11 December 1941, a topic often mentioned in his letters.

He never knew that he had been raised to the rank of Lieutenant Colonel.

My mother always rejected plans to visit the memorial in Tobruk to pray. She did not want to see the monument. She opposed the transfer of her husband's body to the memorial; she wanted him to rest in the idyllic cemetery in Derna.

Index

Index

Index

Index

Index